DARK HORSES

The Magazine of Weird Fiction

JANUARY | 2024

No. 24

Copyright © 2024 Hobb's End Press. All Rights Reserved. Published by Hobb's End Press, a division of ACME Sprockets & Visions. Cover design Copyright © 2024 Wayne Kyle Spitzer. All stories Copyright © 2024 by their respective authors. Please direct all inquiries to: HobbsEndBooks@yahoo.com

CONTENTS

BAD PATIENT
Colton Scott Saylor

WITHOUT SCARS
Jhon Sánchez

NOT A CAT GUY
Cassandra O'Sullivan Sachar

AUTUMNAL EQUINOX REDUX
Will Lennon

A REIGN OF THUNDER
Wayne Kyle Spitzer

TECHNOLUTION
Eleanor Mourante

OF TWO MINDS
Marco Etheridge

EASY ANSWERS
Diana Olney

MECHANICAL DINNER
Nathaniel Barrett

TO THE MEGALITHS OF MONSTROSITY AND BEYOND
D.G. Ironside

BAD PATIENT

Colton Scott Saylor

Up and down and sideways they crawl, and those absurd, unblinking eyes are–

A series of ghostly knocks interrupted Taggert's third attempt at reading the rest of the passage. He rose to the bedroom door, donned his facemask, and cracked the entry. Greeting him with little fanfare was a solitary bowl of cubed beef and cooked vegetables. Dinner time.

The meal had arrived in the usual way: at 6:25PM, on the dot, he would hear a series of small pats on the stairs evolve into deeper, duller wops on carpet before echoing towards the double-doored master bedroom. Three knocks followed, syncopated each night into some new measure of time at the precise moment the plate contacted the floor. Tag would then give his jailer a polite ten second head start (faster wops trailing away) before donning his face mask and shuffling to the doorknob to enjoy his brief glimpse of the "outside world."

Each time, he would afford himself a new object of scrutiny. Upon this present excursion, he lingered on the photo of Sam and him locked in a lover's embrace at Huntington Beach. It wasn't either of their faces that he stared at–it was the ocean.

His glance stolen, he would bend over, pluck his meal from the floor, and step back inside. During those first few deliveries, his fleeting moment of freedom would be accompanied by Sam calling up some cheerful announcement from the landing, anything from "Enjoy!" to the fanciful "Bon appetit!" Tonight, she went with the always in-fashion "Eat up, Bessie!"

Every night, for the past five days, this ceremony played itself out, give or take those few variables. By this time, both performers knew their steps to the second. It was a delicate dance of ergonomics. Not a single calorie wasted.

Once safely at his makeshift desk, Tag appraised tonight's meal: beef stew, complete with carrots, potatoes, cherry tomatoes, and cooked kale that he was certain still had aphids boiled into its dark emerald leaves. He remembered browning the meat for this very dish a week and a half ago, back when his lungs still felt functional and his nose wasn't an endless carousel of mucous. He'd posited that day to Sam as his point of contraction. Perhaps, he had reasoned, one of his neighbors had chosen that exact moment to point a rogue sneeze in his direction? Maybe, he had not-so-subtly hinted, it was Sam's own neighbor friend Clarissa, the soccer-mom extraordinaire who saw fit to latch herself to his wife and drag them into every suburban mundanity imaginable (standing brunch appointments, BBQs where her husband babbled about sports teams Tag felt pressured to fake knowledge of, etc.).

What he hadn't told Sam was the real reason he was currently locked in their bedroom: lunch with Carline. She had been texting him off and on during those spare moments when her own husband had been in the next room, checking to see if

Tag was okay, asking if he could find time to chat. He had impressed himself with his restraint at first, the way he had so quickly deleted her messages as they came in, all the while smiling up at Sam milling about in the kitchen. Eventually, however, he found himself explaining that he needed to take a drive, mumbling something about keeping the battery charged and needing a "mental refresh."

Given his current situation, he lamented that his final rendezvous with Carline had been so chaste: a packed lunch they shared in his car, complete with muted conversation and just a hint of contact between fingers. There had been that kiss at the end, a reminder of better days that had lingered on his lips until he had parked in his driveway.

But since their secret outing, Carline had gone off the map. Every call he made went straight to voicemail, every clandestine text unanswered. At first, he found himself strangely depressed. Theirs was never meant to be anything serious, and yet Tag found that he missed the way Carline had made him feel: desired, respected. The silver lining-Tag prided himself on always finding the positive-was that he finally had the push he needed to block her number from his contacts permanently. He could make a fresh start with Sam, hit a new level in his career. He didn't need Carline or the way she made him feel for any of that.

His banishment to his bedroom had initially put a stop to all that optimism, but in classic fashion, Tag could already see the opportunity hiding in the setback. Perhaps some solitude was just what he needed to re-launch his life. At the very least, he needed space from Sam. Despite her attempt to put a happy face on his quarantine, he knew that his wife still carried some resentment for the way she had found out that he was sick. The first day, it had been nothing but a tickle in the throat, a blip on his otherwise optimal everyday health that he had chalked up to allergies. Looking back, the idea was absurd; he had never had allergies in his life. And yet, his brain had kicked into denial mode with such efficiency that he hardly noticed when the scratch had turned into a sharp pain. It was only after Sam had caught him in the bathroom blowing through his tenth straight tissue that things came to a breaking point. She had been, in a word, enraged.

"I visited my father yesterday, Taggert. A seventy-five-year-old diabetic!"

"How could I have known I was this sick! I felt fine a few days ago. Besides, if it had gotten any worse, I was going to tell you."

This was untrue. His actual plan, once it had become impossible to refuse his situation, had been to let the thing pass without telling her, a demonstration that what the media was bombarding them with on a daily basis was in fact a minor health set-back. If Sam got sick, all the better. She needed to confront how afraid she was. In the deepest reaches of his brain, the places he kept hidden from her but nurtured on his own, he knew he was doing her a favor.

He needled at the dish for a few more minutes, all the while counting the clip clops of his wife's slippers on their hardwood floor downstairs. By this time, she was likely shuttling her own meal to the coffee table just in time for any one of the shows she could enjoy without the pleasure of his cynical commentary. There were only so many Real Housewives of... jokes he could make in one sitting before Sam was ready to throw more than just the remote at his head. Yes, in many ways, this isolation was the best thing for their marriage.

Or at least the best thing for her.

Tag swallowed the thought along with his overcooked beef as broth dribbled down his chin and onto his lap.

"I'm losing it."

"Well, this time to yourself certainly hasn't helped your appearance any. You look awful, Tag, like fucking roadkill."

Joseph–never Joe, not even to his own mother–was sitting in his back office, a sign that business was slower than usual, seeing as how it was one in the afternoon. Tag could spot the mountains of receipts and torn paperwork encroaching from either side of the webcam's frame.

"You don't get it-she won't even let me go out for a walk. I've been in this room since last Sunday."

"That's gotta be borderline abuse. I mean, what's the spousal version of kidnapping?" Joseph's words flew from either side of the cigarette he was lighting up. Tag rolled his eyes just enough for his friend to catch his intent. "Give me a break, okay? I'm in hot water over here. The shutdown is screwing with my bottom line. Did you know I had every author cancel on me last month? The whole reading series for October, down in flames. This hairline is brand new, I'll tell you that."

Joseph bent down to reveal the thinning patch of black and gray acting as a vanguard on his burgeoning forehead. When he glanced back up, his similarly salt and pepper-ed goatee filled Tag's screen. Bits of an old sandwich hung on his friend's whiskers above the lips. Had his appetite not already been gutted by days of illness, Tag might have been repulsed.

"Well smoking out your first editions isn't going to help," Tag replied. "And I need to get back out there before my own losses get any worse."

Their friendship had been defined in part by their mutual dependency: Taggert, adept as he was at tracking down rare books and other antiquities from people who initially did not seem keen to part with their wares, lacked the proper channels to truly make a profit from them while Joseph, terminally indelicate with other's feelings, possessed that shark-gene necessary to peddle limited editions that would cost the average consumer half of their savings.

"It's been how long since you stopped showing symptoms?"

Taggert did the math in his head. "Two days. Temperature's been back and forth, but I feel good. Really good." This was an exaggeration-getting up to piss at night still left him winded and he had a bout of vertigo any time he turned his head too fast–but he was set on speaking his recovery into reality.

"She needs to know that the time you're spending up there in your makeshift ICU is time you guys aren't making any money. Her proofreading K-Mart paperbacks isn't paying the bills. At some point, you have to recognize that you're both letting fear control you."

Tag sucked in air, a reflex he had developed anytime he was avoiding saying the quiet part aloud to his wife. Realizing, however, that she wasn't there to hear his betrayal, he continued, although a bit cautiously: "Not my fear. Hers."

Joseph threw his hands up. "Yours, hers, whatever. On paper, it still looks the same. And if you're not scared, what's stopping you from just walking out?"

Tag breathed in, trying not to notice the effort it took to swallow a modicum of the oxygen that he wanted. The truth was that he had tried to leave, had engaged via video chat in a louder than intended back and forth about what he called her "odd Florence Nightingale power trip."

Ten days, Tag, she had said. Just stay in there for ten days. Ten days of caring about the well-being of anyone other than yourself. Then you can bust out and do whatever the fuck you want. Sam had turned her camera off then, a sign he took to mean that she didn't want him to see her crying. They had paused their communications for some time after that, save for the ritualistic food deliveries. He had promised himself to give her another day to calm down before making his case again.

Joseph's voice flung him back into the present. "Hello? Can you hear me? God, your connection is always dogshit."

"I'm here," Tag reassured him, "it's just not that easy. You don't have someone who'll put up with you enough to stick around; it's a balancing act. I want to have a marriage after this is over."

"See if she sticks around when the checking account hits zero. See if any woman would stick around for that."

"Jesus man, you can be a bit of a prick, you know that?" Tag said in a tone that failed to mask his agreement with his friend.

Joseph smiled, revealing every crooked tooth in his mouth.

Breakfast the next morning was served promptly at 8:00AM. He knew Sam liked to get a jump on her copyediting projects by 8:30 at the latest, meaning she would have at least a half hour of sipping her Chai tea latte in front of her laptop before video-conferencing with her team at the publishers. This meant a brisk but careful walk-run flight up the stairs with Tag's single cup of herbal tea along with a rotating side of fruit (apple, orange, or banana).

He had petitioned for coffee on the day his headaches and coughs had subsided, but Sam had held fast on no caffeine. For not the first time that quarantine, he had felt like a prisoner begging for rations. And for not the first time, Sam had responded like a good warden would: "No, and that's final. Tea for now. Once you're out and about, we'll talk about coffee." She had also mentioned something about the benefits of green tea vs coffee in terms of immunity benefits, but Tag had stopped listening at that point.

This morning, staring at the luke-warm tea on the side table, he felt no desire for breakfast. Like most things he tried to enjoy during this bout of illness, it turned out that his morning meal was also contextual. Tea, coffee, a croissant perhaps, they were all things to hold in one's hand while enjoying the clicks, clacks, spouting steam, and muffled conversation of the cafe. Being out, like a goddamn adult–that's what he missed. Here, in their floral and pastel-laden bedroom that Tag had erroneously let his wife decorate (the deal had been for his study to be truly his study, complete with the dark-leathered trimmings and the required nautical painting), he was a child playing grown-up. And what was worse, attempting to recreate these moments of small happiness he had carved out in his otherwise stressful adult life was only reminding him just how forced and performed those moments of bliss were in the first place.

Tag sat in his office chair, grimacing at the offending mug of tea and overly ripe banana in front of him, when the doorbell downstairs chimed. After a brief pause (perhaps to set down her own mug and to stop whatever cat video she was enjoying on her phone), he heard his wife journey from the dining room to the front door. The familiar clicks of the locking mechanism opening to the outside gave him the briefest imagined sensation of sunshine filling the downstairs entry-way. He waited to hear any hint of conversation pierced with Clarissa's shrill laughter or even the ruffling of plastic that might have been a delivery of early morning groceries. Instead, there was silence, followed by his wife's footfalls pacing from the door. Then, his phone sprung to life. A photo of Sam's face filled the call screen.

"What is it?" He didn't bother with any niceties. They both knew what he was asking about.

"I don't know. Some kind of package. All it has is your name. Not even an address. Like someone just wrapped whatever it is up and plopped it on our porch."

"How big is it?"

"If you're asking if it's a book, I don't know. It's big, heavy too. I'll need to put it in the garage to air it out."

This was her instated protocol for all in-coming packages since his illness: any missives from the outside were given time to "decontaminate" in the garage before gracing their household.

"If it's for me, I'd much rather look at it now. It could be for work, and if that's the case, I'll need to get it unpackaged and stored away sooner than later..."

"No one's opening it. Whatever it is, it'll be fine to wait for 24 hours."

Tag decided to push a bit further than he had planned for this morning. "But if I could get a leg up on getting back to work now, while I'm feeling better–"

"But you're not feeling better," Sam interrupted, exasperated. "At least not yet. And even if this is for work, I can't just bring it in. Help me out here, Taggert. If we both get sick, what then?"

The sharpness with which she uttered his name reminded Tag that they were still in a stalemate from their previous row. He didn't feel up to calming those waters just yet, so he met her coldness with just a hint of annoyance.

"Well if it's addressed to me, can you at least show me a picture?" He had never received a book through the mail, let alone had one mysteriously delivered, but he felt weirdly obligated to dig his heels in regardless.

"I have a meeting to get to, but I'll send up a pic later if I have time. For right now, it's getting stored in the garage. How's your breakfast?"

"Great," he lied. "You know, I'll be ready to come down and help out soon. You'll be able to get more work done once you don't have a patient to look after."

Her sighing filled the receiver, sending a quick pulse of anger into Tag's fingers. "Just one day, Tag, of you not fighting me. Just one."

The smallest hint of regret crept up his neck—he had pushed her a bit too far into a fight he wasn't ready for. Sensing her immediate eruption, he forged a tactical retreat. "I'm sorry, Sam. Just starting to get restless. I am feeling better, but I know you said another week. Ten days. I can do ten days." He could not do ten days, would not, but for now, he just wanted to see the package. "You go to work and send me the picture later. I'll ask Joseph if he knows what it could be in the meantime."

"You do that. Lunch is at 12:15."

Neither of them bothered to say goodbye before the call ended.

That night dinner came on time, the same over-cooked stew along with a tangerine plucked from the tree outside. Tag considered whether or not the addition of citrus was meant as a peace offering. He ate the olive branch, if that's what it was, first, needing anything to brighten his palate before digging into the main course. Downstairs, he heard his wife stack some unknown ceramic atop an alien hard surface to the accompaniment of running water.

While he ate, he stared at his phone, waiting for Joseph to return his call. As he did, he thought of the package, sitting amongst the other forgotten boxes of household supplies and dry goods they had decided to store in the garage like some overstock warehouse. The call never came. When he was finished, he rinsed the bowl in his bathroom sink as he had done the previous nights, then donned his mask and cracked the door open enough to slide the empty dish and silverware out into the hall.

He was just about to crumple onto his mattress when his cell buzzed to life. Tag snatched the phone from the night stand, eager to see if his friend had decided to call him back, only to have his hopes crushed at the sight of his wife's picture fill the screen. He let out one big gust of air, blinked hard, and pushed the accept button.

"You don't usually call for a review of the meal. Is this a new feature of dinner service?" he joked, hoping to charm her into a lighter mood.

"Tag," Sam's voice was low and harsh, "Tag, are you the one talking?"

"What do you mean? You called me, babe. Who else do you think could answer this phone?" Tag replied, chuckling. The irony that it was Sam who had decided to lose her grip on reality and not the person doomed to stare at the same four walls was not lost on him.

His wife's response was in that same hard whisper, every syllable resembling a gasp of air. "That's not what I mean. Was it you just now in the garage?"

"I have no idea what you're talking about. I haven't gone anywhere, Sam. You should know that better than anyone."

"Jesus, okay, I get it, you're sick of being in the room, but I'm being serious right now. I heard someone talking, and it sounded like it was coming from the garage."

"Do you still hear it?" Already, Tag's mind was piecing together the various strands of yarn that it would take for this scare to lead to his freedom. Tag, the Protector. This can work. "Do you want me to check it out?"

There was a pause on the other end of the line as his wife contemplated the offer. Eventually, he heard her footsteps make their way from the kitchen to the laundry room. "It's fine. I don't hear anything right now. It was probably the TV or something."

"Sam, if you're scared, there's no point in not checking it out."

"It's fine, Tag, forget I said anything. Just forget it."

"But-"

"I shouldn't have called. I'm sorry. And I'm sorry that this has been so hard on you. I promise it hasn't been a picnic for me either. I didn't think this was going to be so difficult. I didn't think it had to be."

And with that, her voice cut out. Tag stared at the screen for a while longer, still not believing how close he had come to talking his way out of the room. Once that disbelief had passed, he pondered at how exhausted his wife had sounded. *She's losing it. Sooner or later, she'll need me back. It's only a matter of time.*

Tag was awakened by the earth collapsing beneath him.

The first thing his brain was able to register was the vibrating empty flower vase set on the dresser across from him. Below, the bed was shaking as if someone had placed hydraulics under the mattress. The entire episode came and went too quickly for Tag to be truly afraid or even surprised. Rather, he scanned from one corner of the bedroom to the other, seeking any sign that what he was observing was actually real, that he wasn't still locked in some deep level of dreaming. The thing to truly plunge him back into the waking world was the scream–it was high-pitched and bloody, a sharp wail followed by gurgling as if the source had been plunged into water.

Tag leapt from the mattress on shaky legs and crept to the door. Automatically, his arm shot out for the mask but paused just before yanking it from the perch. Instead, he stood still, wanting to mine any sort of noise from the new-found silence that had smothered the house.

After a few minutes more, he pulled back from the door and surveyed his surroundings. Nothing had been knocked over, and there were no glaring cracks in the drywall. Likely, whatever minor quake had woken him had barely registered on the Richter scale. His thoughts went back to the scream, to the possibility of Sam being injured, and that idea too seemed foolish.

She must have been frightened by the earthquake, he reasoned. *I'd hear from her by now if it had been worse.*

He considered masking up and going to check on her, playing the valiant husband breaking all the rules to ensure that his partner was safe, but no version of the scenario seemed favorable. All he could see was Sam's twisted, angry face upon spying him out of his quarantine. No, he concluded. Better to wait it out. He opted for a phone call, knowing that she was unlikely to answer. At the very least, she'd have seen that he was calling to check on her.

"Just wanted to make sure you were doing okay with the quake. Small potatoes, but it made me miss having you in bed. I love you, Sam." And he did, in that moment, love her. *I'll get out of here soon, get back to work. Everything will go back to how it was. We'll be normal.*

He was thinking through his normal life with all of its trimmings when he fell back asleep.

The next morning, 8:00AM came and went with no knock. A brief glimpse through the cracked open door confirmed it: no breakfast.

Tag didn't see this as suspicious at first: Sam was punctual, yes, but given the earthquake the night before and their argument that had preceded it, he didn't expect the five-star treatment from his wife.

I was sick of that tea anyways, he thought, as he settled down for another morning round of news articles. Once his browser was open, Tag heard a chime from below. Clarissa. She often popped by unannounced in the mornings for a socially-distanced chat once her kids had begun their day of remote-learning. The bell rang a second time before he heard the front door swing slowly open. A muffled high-timbre greeting swept through the downstairs and brushed against his door. Not in the mood to listen to his wife confront their neighbor's passive aggressive taunts, Tag turned back to his laptop.

For the next hour, he scanned a series of news articles and opinion pieces, scouring for just one that he might be able to show to Sam later on as proof that things were being blown out of proportion. The padded reverberations of the two women walking through the house played on as background music.

During his attempt to read an op-ed on "The New Normal," he couldn't help but notice that Clarissa's visit had seemed to alter his wife's typical morning routine. He no longer heard the dulled throb of ditzy YouTube personalities or morning news banter. There were no scrapes or clacks to signal Sam hard at work fixing herself breakfast. Instead, Tag heard something new: stomping, loud and deep, moving from one end of the living room, which was directly beneath the master bedroom, to the other. The thuds emanating from these steps had the muted but bass-heavy womp of something wide and powerful ramming into a flat surface. He conjured up the image of an elephant making its way from one side of his house to the other, and then quickly dismissed it, paranoid that even the thought might make its way somehow to Sam.

She sounds pissed, he thought. And to make matters worse, she seemed in the mood to ensure that Tag knew just how pissed she was. This was new behavior, but still not unexpected. His careless needling the other day had been a miscalculation. Between that and what must have been a frustrating visit with Clarissa, his chances at getting out today seemed slim to none.

He was still planning out the series of off-hand comments and targeted shows of gratitude he'd have to drop to get back into Sam's good graces this evening when his laptop lit up. With one click, Joseph popped onto his desktop. His evergreen scowl was replaced with a cheshire grin that only seemed reserved for moments of windfall.

"Morning sunshine," Joseph yelped, rotating back and forth in his office chair with disconcerting energy.

"What's got you in such a dapper mood?" Tag asked, conscious of his own frazzled and thinning hair that was likely revealing patches of scalp he'd rather no one see. He attempted to run his hands through the mess in an effort to cover the gaps.

"Who loves you, you bastard? I wanna hear you say it."

"What the fuck are you talking about?"

Joseph's beaming face faltered only slightly. "Don't be coy with me. Thanks to my generosity, you're back in business."

Tag finally stopped fretting over his grizzled appearance and focused on Joseph's screen. "I have no idea what you're talking about."

"You didn't receive any mail yesterday?"

In the midst of the quake business from the night before, Tag had forgotten all about calling Joseph to ask about the package. "So that was you."

"Well, sort of. I had some kid come in wanting to denote a book. Didn't even want cash for it: he just said he wanted to get rid of it and that my shop was the first place he found on the web. And the book is legit. He only let me glance at it, but I know enough to know it's something rare. I figured I'd do you a solid and send him your direction, see what you thought about it. Told him some line about needing my colleague to do the appraisals and that he works from home."

Tag massaged the bridge of his nose, trying to piece together the disparate bits of data he was hearing. "Who even was this guy?"

"Never seen him before. The kid looked like some new-money techie dipshit. You know the type, right?"

Tag gave a nod, thinking of all the Tesla-driving nouveau-riche he and Joseph had duped in the past just so that these same schmucks could line their office shelves with books that cost the same as a small house. "I'm aware, yes."

"Well, he mentioned getting the book from his grandfather's will. He said he wanted it out of his place as soon as possible."

"Who's the grandfather?"

"Didn't say, but I was curious so I looked into it. Only geezer I know who bit the dust recently was some energy mogul who lived up in the hills. Real old money, like slave-labor-likely-paid-for-some-of-this-guy's furniture-old money. And if it's the same person, you're in for a nice surprise."

"Why's that?" Tag asked, not bothering to hide his annoyance at how long Joseph was dragging this out.

"This particular old geezer had a side hobby in rare editions. He has a lot of plaques in a lot of very large museums and libraries. So imagine what kind of off-the-wall stuff he saved for himself? And if this kid is attached to this estate, my guess is that this first book is just a taste of the larger nut. What I'm really trying to say is: don't fuck this up."

Tag swallowed hard, a mix of excitement and dread congealing in his stomach. Never had such a great opportunity seemed to come at a worse time. Whatever black magic he would need to conjure to get out of this prison, he would have to do it soon.

"So you gave him my address?" Tag didn't mean for the question to sound as accusatory as it did.

"Yup. Thought I was doing you a favor. I figured if Sam sees how valuable you being back at work can be, she'd give a little."

"Sam saw it alright. It's in the garage now." Tag thought for a second before asking, "Did the kid mention anything about the book?"

"Not really," Joseph replied, clearly annoyed that Tag wasn't showering him with gratitude. "Just said he wanted it gone. I didn't want to spook him anymore than he already looked, so I didn't press. Look man, are you gonna retrieve your balls and make good on my gift, or what?"

"Just give me a few more days. I know what I'm doing."

Before Joseph could reply, Tag flashed over the "end call" button and clicked. He stared at his gaunt face in the screen reflection for a bit before flipping it closed. Heavy footsteps sounded from the room just below the stairs. He could hear puffs of breath between each stomp and imagined his wife as a petulant child, clutching her ears and exhaling angrily. Just as the image sent a small smile across his face, the noises stopped. On the floor below, all was quiet once more.

Come 12:30PM, he swiped his phone's screen, awaiting his wife's lunch signal to flash beneath his hand. However, the text never came. By 1:15PM, his confusion had transformed into a satisfying, righteous anger.

"I need to eat, honey!" he called out from his mattress. He wasn't sure how well she could hear with the door closed, which gave him license to throw more venom into the shout. He paused in anticipation for more angry stomping, but the silence persisted. *Fucking child*, he thought as he started to the door. When his hand pawed the doorknob, he caught his spare arm already grasping for the mask. Tag stood there for a moment before whispering "Fuck that." Resolute, he turned the knob and stuck his head into the hallway.

An odd smell hit his face as soon as he leaned outwards. It was the scent of musk and mold, like coming across damp clothing set aside for a few weeks. Tag's face tightened into disgust. *Has the house smelled like this the entire time? How much did that mask filter out?*

He peered towards the stairs and shouted, "Sam! I said I need to eat, babe!"

A loud thump resonated from below, which he identified as the doorway leading to the garage. *Must not have heard me*, he reasoned.

Not wanting Sam to arrive and catch him maskless, he closed the door and receded to the bed. *There, I'm nice and compliant. A good dog waiting for his meal.*

But the meal didn't come. Instead, the noises below continued, a series of muffled thuds like someone boxing a hunk of beef. He leaned back onto the bed, waiting for the violent symphony to stop. Just then, a rogue thought sent a stab of panic into the base of his neck. Had Carline finally decided to self-destruct and call Sam? It made too much sense. This sudden wave of fury could only have been explained by Sam finally figuring out where Tag had been during those supposed "Out-of-town buyer trips." But his wife's silence made less sense. She wouldn't have been able to resist unloading her fury on him for this long. He waited there, hands nervously clutching at each other.

She doesn't know anything. This will pass. Pretty soon, you'll be back outside, and Sam will be back to normal. He pawed at the thought with careful optimism.

Just then, three explosive knocks shook the door to his bedroom, each of them harnessing the concentrated force of a hammer striking a nail. Tag jolted up, adrenaline surging through his legs even as his vision began tunneling from rising too quickly. He waited for the rush of blood to finish its work before he crept to the source of the noise.

"Sam?" The frustration had left his voice and been replaced by timid curiosity. "Sam, what's wrong?" There was no reply.

He evaluated the door, waiting for the knocks to come again. Somewhere in that waiting, his body began drifting closer to the doorway. Before he knew it, his ear was pressed against the cold wood, searching for any evidence that his wife was there on the other side. At first, all he heard was the suction of his eardrum pinned to the surface. Then, beneath the sullen quiet, he heard it. Breathing, no, panting, the ragged exhales you hear from a dog trying to keep cool in the summer.

"Sam?"

At no point did he consider opening the door. Since the knocks had come, the atmosphere in the house had changed. Everything felt wound three turns too tight, a world of taunt piano strings.

"Sam, is that yo-" Before he could finish, a hideous thump landed at the place where his head was pressed to the door. He felt the compressed power meet the wood and reverberate into his skull even as he was launching himself away from the frame. His body tucked into what might have passed for a tactical roll that, when finished, left him kneeling on one already swelling knee.

He knelt and listened to his own ragged breath, daring the door to move.

As he waited, Tag's lower body pulsed in agony. The pain allowed his righteous indignation to return with new vigor. What gives her the right to act like this anyway? The anger started to eat away at the sharper edges of his fear. As if to perform the finishing blow, his mind flashed, That bitch. The statement was the kind that would never have left his lips, but there, on the precipice of his upstairs hall, it was a talisman.

No fucking right.

He was properly amped by the time his hand found the knob and twisted. The space that greeted him looked the same as the last time he had peered from his cage, from the thick blue carpet to the smattering of framed photos strung on either wall. But as he began to step into the hallway, Tag's foot struck something solid. A cry of surprise escaped from his mouth as he jerked his head down.

At first he didn't recognize the object at his feet. It was large and oval-shaped, doused in a pale green that even in the dim light looked sickly. Tag blinked in confusion before his mind caught up with his senses: it was the dish they kept on the table for any of the odd kick-knacks that get acquired over the course of life in a fairly disorganized household. There in the hall, the dish looked to be in bad shape. The edge of the platter was chipped, leaving a jagged point that looked sharp enough to draw blood. That must have been why, he reasoned, the belly of the container was doused in scarlet. Jesus, she cut herself.

"Sam, Christ, are you hurt?" He hated the surge of hope that had welled up inside of him along with the recognition that Sam's injury was the perfect way for him to leave his quarantine. "This has gone on far enough now–we're going to the ER."

Two things stopped Tag from re-attempting his exit onto the second-floor landing. One of them was a second, more discerning glance at the platter, which he finally realized was filled with a bleeding lump of meat. He couldn't place what cut of beef would have been that misshapen, that fresh. The second thing that paused his leg mid-step was the noise he heard welling from the downstairs living room. It started as a faint patting, the kind you hear from kids at a birthday table when somebody calls for a drumroll. Before long, the pitter-patters transformed into what Tag could only consider a full-on gallop, the sound of something running on more than two limbs. The flaps of appendages slapping hardwood caused his spine to go rigid. He stayed there, frozen in the half-open doorway as the noise grew louder and louder. A squeaking followed by an abrupt change in the pounding signaled that something was turning in the hall that led from the dining room towards the staircase. A few seconds more, and it would be appearing from the stairs leading to where he stood.

Run, you fucking idiot, some voice in the deepest part of his gut shrieked, and then Tag was heaving himself back into the bedroom. From his new vantage point on the carpet, he saw with horror that he had forgotten to close the door. The platter of bleeding flesh-he could think of no other name for meat that raw-was still sitting there. The galloping was much louder now, as if the thing were skipping three steps at time in order to meet him.

With speed he might never be able to conjure again, Tag shot out his right foot and kicked at the ajar door. It slammed shut, blocking out the awful hallway with the rancid stench. As it did, he was already up and throwing himself at the wood, hand scrambling for the lock on the knob. Then the galloping thing was throwing itself at the door, this time not bothering to focus its rage on any one singular point. As a result, the slams were awful, meaty slaps that resembled a body smacking concrete with all limbs pulled back. More than once, Tag was sure he heard something splinter, be it wood or bone.

"Sam, please, stop!" He wasn't sure why he was still yelling his wife's name. No part of him registered the presence in his hallway as Sam, the same petite blonde that he had once picked up and spun around with one wrapped arm during their first dance as a married couple. Between each gruesome slam, he registered those same heavy, animalistic breaths along with a low screeching that had no business emanating from human vocal chords.

"Sam, I'm sorry, okay?" His voice sounded terrified and ashamed.

He heard the sound of clattered porcelain, followed by one final shove at the door that lacked the animosity, the hunger, from earlier. Then, the many-limbed thing meandered back down the hall.

Tag sat crying on the carpet for a minute more, waiting to hear the intruder retreat all the way back into some deeper part of the house. But it didn't. The steps continued down the stairs and then froze, lingering at the bottom with palpable anticipation. He sat stunned, not knowing whether or not it was safe to move. His brain struggled to piece together any semblance of logic, any even semi-believable explanation for what was waiting for him downstairs. That was when the training his body had undergone since the start of his quarantine kicked in. The knocks, the dish...

It wants me to eat, he realized. It's dinner time.

Burdened by shaking hands, Tag crawled back to the door. He edged it open and slid the bowl of gore into his bedroom. Downstairs, he heard a small coo of approval.

Once his tremors had stopped, Tag tried to call 911. As the phone rang, he sized up the bloody mess at the center of the dish once more. Its edges were so ragged that it looked as if it had been chewed rather than carved. He wondered if the Intruder-that was what he had decided to call the nameless thing-was downstairs waiting to hear him shout down his approval at its delivered meal. All the while, the phone continued to ring. Frustrated, Tag hung up and tried the number again. As his fingers went to dial, however, he noticed the symbol in the top left corner of his phone: zero bars. A swell of anxiety began in his lower abdomen, like small animals chewing on his intestines.

Trying to outpace his panic, he leaped to his laptop. The loading-icon mocked him with its infinite rotation.

Had the Intruder found a way to jam his cell phone signals? At the very least, it must have known enough to unplug the wireless router, which he had unfortunately decided to place in the downstairs living room. Not a chance I could make it down there in one piece to plug it back in.

Next, he surveyed the window overlooking the backyard, which was just beginning its march into pale blue shadow. He could barely make out the interior of the yards on either side of his perimeter fences; neither held any evidence of a neighbor out for a casual jaunt around the property. The house directly behind him was awash in darkness. Just as he was beginning to lose hope, a flicker of light the size of a small flame appeared from the yard behind his. Looks like a match.

In an instant, Tag was clawing at the latch to his right desperate to get the person's attention. The frigid outside air revealed a neighborhood aghast with the typical white noise: a distant dog forever barking, some screeching set of tires peeling out of a red light, wind meeting leaves. Tag readied his body and let loose a cracked peal.

"Someone! Anyone, please! Someone fucking help me!"

His ears perked at the sound of rustling from the yard in front of him. Emboldened, he forced himself to yell once more. "Someone, please, I'm trapped in here! I'm-"

He stopped at the sight of two bright bulbs floating in the growing dark near his back fence. Not a match at all. They look like phone lights, he thought, and he clawed with animal abandon at the possibility. They did, in fact, look like two hands simultaneously holding their phones aloft, perhaps attempting to peer over the fence to locate the origin of the cries. Tag cocked back to deliver another painful scream when his vision caught something else in the twilight. More shining surfaces beneath the lights, like an array of broken glass held before a disco ball.

The two lights blinked in tandem and then narrowed.

Tag's innards imploded. The row of shattered mirrors widened further, curving upward into a sickening smile. He stepped back from the window. As he did, the odd collage of shapes cohered into two glowing eyes nestled atop a sickening grin of knives. And somewhere beneath that face, Tag saw the vague outline of a body standing just in front of the fence, a mockery of angles and limbs, everything ending at a point and ready to tear.

It was waiting for me... It wants me to know I'm in a cage.

A low growl from below him rang in response.

Tag spent that evening sitting between the wall and his bed-it was as close as he could get to throwing himself underneath the mattress, which would have been his preferred hiding spot. The Intruder, meanwhile, had been quite busy. From the moment he had backed away from the window, it had gone to work on the downstairs, prowling from room to room like a silverback surveying its new territory. Once that initial pacing had ceased, Tag heard new sounds: snapping wood, cracking of porcelain and glass. Initially, he allowed himself the faint hope that the clamor would alert one of his neighbors, but after several more hours, that hope vanished.

He imagined the Intruder racing through each room, leaving a trail of broken furniture and shattered family heirlooms in its wake. At some point, however, he began to sense a pattern in the chaos. It wasn't prowling randomly from one end of the house to the other; rather, it was running a circuit. First, it would approach the front parlor before moving to the adjacent dining room. Once those two points were cleared, it would enter the kitchen before finally ending up in the family room. In each space, he heard a series of cracks and snaps along with the sound of dragging debris. The lap would eventually terminate in the same spot every time: the garage.

He pondered what it could be doing with all of their belongings, a spare thought that finally reminded him of something that had been pushed aside when the terror had started.

Sam. Part of Tag had instantly come to terms with his wife's death upon that first slam against the door. Since then, he had slipped into a survivor mode that he never imagined he was capable of, the sort of sheer narcissism that it felt like he had been training for his entire life. Now, in what amounted to some kind of calm, he was shocked at his lack of grief. Sam was gone, but in a way, all of the world outside of his room was equally no longer present. He was a man apart, a soul on a deserted island surveilled by one lone, hungry shark.

I'm alone here. I'm all I have. He tried to allow the steady beating of talons against hardwood to lull him to sleep.

Outside, the moon burned, pale and angry.

He awoke at 8:25AM to the sound of ringing.

Tag staggered to his feet, muscles shouting from the awkward angles he had forced them into the previous night. An empty burn in his gut reminded him that he had been without food for over a day. The hunger ache tempted him to eye the bloody mess still resting on the floor; it had changed to a dull reddish-brown and taken on the beginning fragrance of rot.

Below him, the dull pounding returned again along with what sounded like a man yelling.

The noise caused a pulse of light to run through Tag's body, a jolt of hope that propelled him to the door. He leaned his body against the entry and rested his right hand on the knob, fingering its round edges.

Where is it?

His mind raced, every nerve seeking out evidence of the Intruder's whereabouts. He considered how long it had taken to move from one room to the next, how many steps it had needed to lope up the stairs to his bedroom. Tag had never possessed what anyone would mistake as an athletic build, but he did currently have what the athletes he had observed in his lifetime lacked: the raw, grinding need for life, that extra ounce of adrenaline that ejects the gazelle from the lion's claws. He felt that power then as the bell returned once more.

C'mon, you fucker.

That was when he heard the clicking of a lock.

"Sam?" The layers of wall and insulation put the voice just on the wrong side of recognizable, but the low register told Tag it was a man. He listened closer, body now shaking so badly that he could feel the knob rattling in his hand.

"Sam, I swung by...house key...check on... guys... to see how Tag was."

Against all cries of preservation from the back of his skull, he allowed himself to turn the knob and allow rotten air into his bedroom. Along with the smell came Joseph's crystal clear call from what must have been the downstairs landing.

"Tag? Is that you up there?"

"Joseph, Jesus, get the fuck out of here." The words emanated in a ragged whisper that seemed to come from his throat. "You need to get out."

He heard Joseph take two steps up the bottom stairs, every sound now a gunshot in the otherwise dead quiet house. Where the hell is it?

"Tag, you're scaring me, man. I've been trying to get a hold of you. Thought I might check on that book." The man took a few more careful steps up the stairway. Tag leaned further out into the hall until he could just make out the tip of Joseph's paunch entering the mid-landing. "Christ, what is that smell?"

"Joseph," Tag called out, his whisper-shouts now evolved into a full on cry, "call 9-11. There's something in the house, an animal or something. I think it killed Sam."

Joseph now stepped fully into view, a picture in a stained lime-green polo shirt and khaki shorts. His hand was covering his face in an attempt to block out the putrid miasma that even now was burning Tag's nostrils.

"Fuck, man, I think all that time in quarantine ha-"

Joseph never got to finish the thought. One instant, he was there chastising Tag; the next, he had vanished from the stairway. The disappearance was so complete that Tag wondered whether or not his friend had been a hallucination, the final sign that he had slipped into full-on madness.

That was when the screams began. They started low, a cluster of growls and grunts, before morphing into a falsetto that seemed to go on forever. In the midst of those shrieks, Tag could just make out something wet flopping onto the floor, a damped mop slapping against the hardwood over and over again, before one quick tearing noise ended everything. He took two more steps out into the hall, cognizant even then that this was the furthest he had gone from his bedroom since the day he had first been locked up. The thought was interrupted by the sound of something heavy and damp being dragged from the bottom of the stairs and back into the belly of the house.

This is it, Tag thought. If it's taking Joseph back into the garage, I'll never have a better shot at the front door. He waited for the sliding to reach the hallway running past the kitchen before he ventured three more steps towards the top of the stairs. Doing so allowed him his first real glimpse at the living room. Before his internment, the room had been an attempt at a minimalist-inspired reading area replete with a sterilized Ikea loveseat, framed prints aping Rothko, and a bookcase filled with unfinished hardcovers. Now, it was a tribute to viscera, an abstract abomination of strewn limbs and coagulated balls of tissue and blood. Along the walls were streaks of brown and red, the two competing hues running in spiraling tracks until they met just behind the overturned and gutted couch. From his position at the entrance of the hall, Tag could just make out one leg jutting from behind the loveseat.

Once his foot hit the first stair, his mind tunneled towards the front door, which still swung barely ajar. Sweeps of sunlight streaked the crimson splatters on the dark wood flooring, revealing new clumps of hair, shit, and organs that rose like tombstones throughout his downstairs.

He began to count out each stair as a way of neglecting the hellscape around him. One step. Two steps. Three steps. When he reached the mid-landing, he noticed new crunches from the hall stretching back towards the garage. No, his brain scolded, keep on the steps. Then the counting came back, but louder this time. **SEVEN STEPS. EIGHT STEPS. NINE STEPS.**

When the sound of a door opening emerged from the back hall, Tag was nearly to the bottom of the stairs. Had he allowed himself a lapse from his steeled gaze on the front door, he might have seen the dim illumination from the garage lighting the darkened space to his right. Instead, he kept his head trained on his escape. When the whoosh of something impossibly fast for its size swept from the shadowed path and brushed against his shoulder, he was still gazing at the exit. It felt as if he had been gently pushed aside by someone walking through a crowd, a casual repositioning. Then the flush of hot, stinking air to his left nearly sent him back onto his ass. Struggling to keep his balance, Tag reached out with his right hand to catch himself. The limb flailed towards the railing, but he had no sensation of his fingers gripping the wood. Confused, he looked down and saw what remained of his arm wagging without purpose. Just below the elbow, he spied a protrusion of white and red bone. For one moment, he simply stared at the remains in wonder before a jet of blood flew from the wound and out towards the already soaked living room.

In front of him, something panted and chewed. The Intruder clicked its claws on the dampened floor and dared him to look up. He refused.

Still dazed, Tag pushed himself further into the back of the house, past the entry to the kitchen, which he noticed with one glimpse was awash with body parts and carved flesh. *My dinner*, his mind chided even as he tore down the hall. He heard the Intruder giving chase behind him, a litany of clicks and screeches on four legs. Tag began turning towards the family room, hoping to make it into the backyard and then, if his blood loss allowed, over his neighbor's fence. Perhaps sensing this plan, he heard the Intruder first tearing through the kitchen entry then sprinting to the back sliding door. He skidded on the wood floor, right arm now erupting with what was left of his life, a crude trail of blood recording his movements. With his remaining arm, he gripped the only means of egress left: the door to the garage.

With the sounds of the Intruder roaring in frustration behind him, he stepped through the door and slammed it shut. Tag worked the lock, a futile gesture that made him feel safer nonetheless. Once the mechanism clicked into place, he spun around-and immediately collapsed. The feeling of his kneecaps slamming onto cement hurt some other version of himself, trapped in a hall of reflecting mirrors some million miles away. The Tag that was bleeding to death in what had once been a cluttered but otherwise perfectly normal garage had no need for those old sensations. What stood before him ripped away any of those mundane trappings of a healthy body at work.

Eight feet tall at least, a pile of broken furniture, kitchen utensils, fire pokers, cracked picture frames. The barrage of debris curved at its apex before spiraling back down to the floor. Holding it all together was a thick, oozing mortar that looked the color of mud mixed with tar. Within some of the cracks, he noticed odd sprinklings of limbs, fingers, and organs. Once his brain fixed on the monolith, it changed before his eyes. No longer was it a pile of his destroyed belongings awash with gore; now, Tag glimpsed what could only be a doorway, a blackened hole at the center bordered by jagged edges of rubbish. The mass in the middle of the gateway swirled in amorphous patterns and pulsed with foul breath. Whenever it exhaled, Tag felt the tether holding his sense of the world tighten to the point of breaking. From somewhere deep beyond wherever the door led, he heard screams married with guttural laughter.

At the foot of the structure, he noticed a large book sprawled open and filled with arcane symbols. The pages of the book were charred at the center, as if someone had lit a match to the paper.

My package.

At the top of the doorway, Tag noticed three broken wooden handles sticking out like spears towards the ceiling. On the outside poles rested the severed heads of Joseph and what could have only been Clarissa, both faces still locked in an eternal cry for more life.

The middle pole was empty.

Behind him, the garage door flung open. In front of him, the portal bulged with the promise of something hideous and infinite begging to be let in.

Tag thought back to his bedroom, to those four walls that held him locked in place and anchored safely to the earth. He found himself wishing to be back in there, eating his wife's miserable stew and guzzling down any tea she found fit to brew.

As he turned toward what breathed behind him, he noticed it was still wearing her gray sweats, even though there was hardly any gray left in that copper-rusted heathered cotton. A grotesque grin opened from behind blood-matted strings of blonde hair.

Tag forced one last smile through his trembling sobs. "I think I'm okay now, honey. I'm feeling much better, I swear."

WITHOUT SCARS

Jhon Sánchez

The woman on the screen wasn't me. She had my face, my body, and was making love with Roberto, but she wasn't me. Her butt had a weird purple scar shaped like a star. *I wish I wasn't looking at these memory recordings.* We watched those memories, so they got stuck in our minds. *How can that scar be there? How come these memories are all mixed up?* At that moment, I didn't care about fertility treatments. I imagined myself running down the hall and yelling that Roberto was a *dog. And I have to confront whatever bitch slept with my husband.* All the people in this clinic would be watching, and the woman who slept with my husband might be among them. I looked away from the screen toward the dark curtains covering the windows. I propped myself back against the bed pillows and took some deep breaths to calm as the screen continued showing that *pornography.*

Roberto was lying next to me, and I wanted to push him out of bed. *Better not.* He sucked my breasts, then lifted away and positioned himself between my legs. I let him in so he would be convinced that the memory recordings were doing the job, that I was docile, that Dr. Silverman was right: "Good memories make you happier, so you can make better love."

The ceiling fan's blades rotated around Roberto's head, and I wished he would transform into a helicopter, detach, flying away from my vagina. I moaned, gasped, and moved my lower body. I imagined him as a compressing piston, hoping he would eject his fluid soon.

My ID bracelet was too tight. I wished I could take it off and leave Roberto and this clinic. I just wanted to get out of there. I felt like vomiting. *Why is this room the same as all the other rooms in this clinic?* The same white bureau, the same light blue curtains. How I wanted to dye them pink and make them my own. I know we'd had a house before coming here, but I couldn't remember it. I found myself in my memory looking up toward the sky, and all I could see was a glass dome as if I were inside a greenhouse.

I looked back at the screen. The woman with the scar was still there. She had finished making love and was now covered with a blanket. I *had* to find that woman. I was determined not to tell Dr. Silverman about my jealousy. I didn't want him to 'update' me, to change out my memory "for something more pleasant," as he would say.

Roberto came inside me and repeated twice with his eyes open, "I want this baby." Dr. Silverman recommended that we keep our eyes open during lovemaking to capture better memories. I assumed the fetal position, put my thumb in my mouth, and closed my eyes with all my strength as if my eyelids could keep the tears from overflowing.

I didn't know how much longer I could pretend that our treatment was going to work. I couldn't remember anything that happened before we got to this clinic except for those events implanted by Dr. Silverman. *Maybe Roberto erased my past, my memories. I thought that Roberto didn't want me to remember something and that's why he had paid for this treatment Was he unfaithful?* It had to be. *Maybe Roberto has some kind of fetish for women with scars.* This seemed weird to me because my skin was absolutely perfect. Not even a single mole. I'd never had acne. No scars. I had heard that men sometimes look for the opposite of what they have at home. But a woman with that horrible scar? I cried in silence and hoped that Dr. Silverman would not erase this moment of pain, this memory that could help me find the bitch.

Roberto whispered in my ear, asking if everything was all right. He noticed something was off but couldn't figure out exactly what the problem was. He knew it, even though I was trying my best to hide my emotions. I pretended to be asleep, and he left me alone.

Minutes later, the shower sounded like a storm over a tin roof. Roberto was inside, probably scrubbing his ankles, the first thing he did when he bathed. Soon, the maids—their faces and heads covered in the same material as their black unitards—would clean up the tufts of our implanted hair that littered the floor, and then we would go for breakfast. I calculated that I barely had five minutes before his shower was up. I turned on the screen and rewound the recording. I wanted to be sure that my eyes hadn't lied to me. The replay was painful, but I needed to know the truth. And I saw it again: my butt with that weird star-like scar.

I clicked on the menu and scrolled down, looking for another scene to watch. I didn't want Roberto to see me watching the sex scene with that woman. He could get suspicious and tell Dr. Silverman. *First Date*, *Marriage*, and *Honeymoon* were listed first. I clicked on *First Date*. These were all recordings of implanted memories.

I never knew how I'd gotten to this clinic. One day, I just woke up in a bed. At that time, I only knew my name, and that I had a husband, Roberto. A nurse made me take a sedative, and Dr. Silverman told me, "You don't have any memory." He took my hand and stroked it, adding, "Trust me. That's good for you and your marriage."

"Why am I here?" I kept asking, disturbed by knowing that I was only a name, Victoria.

"We want you to have happy memories so you can carry happy babies," he said, as if he were talking to a toddler. That made me angry. I grabbed him by the throat and spit on him. The nurses restrained me. I wanted to punch all of them, but the sedative was taking effect. Silverman continued, "Your anger has roots in unconscious events. We can only access them when you're in an agitated state, but the sedative you took is preventing that. We need to erase memories associated with negative emotions."

The next day, Dr. Silverman had brought me to a huge machine that would implant new memories. I thought it was foolish to re-implant something that was already erased. I asked him why.

He replied, "We retouched your memories so you can have a better experience when you remember them."

"Retouched?"

"Like a photograph. We just erased the imperfections."

Reading not only my confusion but the fear on my face, Dr. Silverman said, "Don't worry. It's for your children. You don't want to transmit bad memories to your children." I wanted to have healthy, beautiful, fruit-of-love children, and didn't know that we could transmit memories to them. I understood that Dr. Silverman would implant happy memories of my life events. So, I ended up here, watching memory recordings every day.

I clicked "Start" on the *First Date* recording as Roberto continued showering. Although I liked to watch the recordings, I was angry about that woman with the scar. I thought that Roberto plotted it all. He probably cheated on me and doesn't want me to remember.

I heard a knock-knock on the door. It was likely one of the black lizards—as I called the maids—those sexless creatures with black headcovers.

"Can you wait? He's still in the shower," I yelled. There was no response. *Are they mute?* I didn't think they were forbidden to talk.

I turned off the screen as Roberto came into the bedroom from the shower because *First Date* had ended. He glanced toward the pitch-dark square that now looked like a black mural. When he threw himself down at my side, I was afraid the mattress would explode. I didn't know why I thought this, but it scared me. I grabbed Roberto's wrists so hard that his bracelet ID hurt my palm. My hands were clammy, and I was gasping for breath. I thought that if I lost my grip, I would fall into a huge ditch that was opening underneath the bed. He was starting to fall asleep. I thought about the woman with the scar. I shook him. Wanted to punch him.

The next morning at breakfast, Roberto leaned across our table, kissed me on the neck, and rubbed a grape over my lips. "Ah, that fruit," I said as I looked away from him, scanning the room and wondering who the woman with the scar could be. It could be anyone—one of the other wives, or one of the mothers who were helping to feed their children. All the children seemed to have the same face. I shook my head.

"Is everything okay?" He still held the grape between his thumb and index finger.

"Is today the day we need to go for more hair implants?" I was trying to redirect the conversation. We had gone two days ago, and those implants hadn't fallen out as much. I didn't want him to figure out that I was jealous. He would tell Dr. Silverman.

He ignored me. I breathed in deeply, massaged my neck, and grabbed the grape, swallowing it whole. "Sweet," I lied.

"So, the treatment is working."

I looked at him, trying to understand what he meant. He told me that I used to hate grapes after an aunt forced me to eat a lot of them in childhood.

"Dr. Silverman was successful in erasing that memory," Roberto said, munching some grapes. I saw what looked like a white powder in his mouth. *That* was weird.

The clacking of the cutlery on china along with the din of conversation sounded like a loud concert of cicadas. Anxious, I fidgeted with my bracelet ID, wanting to tear it off despite Dr. Silverman saying that this was impossible. A maid presented me with a tray of hard-boiled eggs. This somehow shifted into what looked like a charcoal-drawn image. Confused, I nodded for the maid to serve me some. Then the woman with the scar entered my thoughts. I massaged my temples and looked at the eggs again. Now they looked almost too white, *too* perfect. I wondered where all this food comes from. I never saw the kitchen, or anyone cooking. *I'm starving, and that bitch took away my appetite. I don't want to eat a thing. Roberto is to blame. He's cheating on me.*

The maid's lips were so hidden by her headcover that they looked like gill slits. *Black lizard.* As she put my bacon on my plate, its grease sparkled so much that I kept blinking as if I were looking at a bright sun. The maid's black gloves and uniform cooled my eyes. Their unitards were so concealing that I realized I had never seen their skin.

A woman three tables away stood up and toppled her table sideways, yelling, "*That* monster is not my child. Kill that creature. Kill it. Where is *my* child?"

A crew of nurses appeared to restrain her while the maids tried to pacify the child.

Dr. Silverman suddenly appeared in the dining room and said, "Continue enjoying your breakfast. It's just another case of resurfacing memories."

I bit into a piece of toast and asked Roberto, "Why do you think women stress out about their children so frequently in the dining room?" He knew I felt that something wasn't right.

He shrugged. "I don't care, as long as I feel happy."

The fact that Roberto cheated on me could cause me to make a scene like that. *He has to be cheating. If only I could remember if he'd done it before! Who could have a scar like that?* I thought about the women I'd seen in the sauna. Wait a minute. They all had perfect skin, round hard hips, and no trace of scars.

I pushed my plate to the side. I was nauseous, so I went to the ladies' room. When I opened the door, I saw a maid washing her hands. What I saw shocked me. Her naked hands under the running water had purple scars, similar to the one I had seen on the woman's butt. Without hesitation, I grabbed the maid by the wrist. I noticed that she didn't have a bracelet ID. I rolled back one of her sleeves, uncovering at least two inches of a scar on that arm, a glossy purple map-like mark. I felt as if I had touched a rat. She took advantage of my revulsion and pushed me to the side, then grabbed her gloves and ran out.

"I have a suspect," I said aloud to myself as I paced back and forth. I was alone in the bathroom, and so continued talking out loud, "But why didn't I take off her headcover? Stupid. It was her. It *had* to be." I made a fist, then ordered myself to take a deep breath. *Why does she have so many scars? And I don't have any. Not even a tiny one.* I wanted to be sure, though. I locked the door and took off all my clothes. I examined every inch of my body. It suddenly struck me that my nose and ears were similar to Roberto's. I spent the most time looking at my butt. The roundness of it, the smoothness of the skin. Smoothness? But when I closed my eyes and touched my butt, my skin prickled as if it were made of shards of glass. *Why do I see something different from what I sense with my fingers? It's like blind people who perceive things around them. My eyes are showing me a smoothness that doesn't exist.*

Once, while we were watching a movie about a blind man, I'd asked Roberto whether we would still love each other if we were blind. I closed my eyes and slid my fingers along the naked thigh below his shorts. His skin felt like tree bark. Stunned, I opened my eyes, asking myself what I was touching. Roberto hugged me and held my face, saying, "Remember what Dr. Silverman said, 'Always make love with your eyes open.'"

"Roberto," I said. "If that's the case, how would blind people make love?"

He laughed so hard he had to hold his stomach. "They only exist in movies."

It was true that there were no blind people in the clinic. I closed my eyes again and started to suck my thumb, the behavior I always did when something bothered me. "But how did that happen? I mean . . . They have to be *somewhere*."

"They're like Superman . . ."

He saw that I was upset and held me by the shoulders, then took my chin and said, "Blindness has been cured. Now open your eyes. I want to see you this way forever."

As I put my clothes back on in the bathroom, I began to think that maybe blindness hadn't been cured at all. The blind were probably working somewhere, just like the maid with the scarred hands. I looked at my hands. They had touched the maid's. Disgusting. The memory of her scarred hands made me vomit into a toilet. After flushing it down, I felt better.

Returning to the dining room, I looked for that maid. But they all looked the same, like black tadpoles in their identical spandex uniforms, gloves, and head coverings. *How could Roberto dare? Cheating with one of these insignificant creatures?*

I had to control myself. I didn't want these particular memories to be removed because they upset me. I inserted my pinky into the space between my bracelet ID and skin and slid it back and forth. I didn't want to have that thing around my wrist.

Thirsty, I approached a crystal fountain containing water and blueberries. As I pressed the dispenser, the glitter of the crystal made me see my reflection as if my entire face, neck, and hands were covered with purple warts. I gasped and dropped my glass. The maids hurried over to wipe up the mess.

Once I stopped shaking, I returned to our table. When a maid came to replace my water, I leaned across to Roberto pretending to play with his neck. I really wanted to monitor his pulse, thinking it would go up if he lied to me. With my fingertip against his artery, I asked him very quietly, "Have you ever wondered about them?"

"The maids, you mean?"

I wanted to say, 'They must be women and they are beautiful, in a way,' but I knew this would set off his alarm bells, and he would accuse me of jealousy. Instead, I said, "We don't know anything about them. We can't even tell which ones are men and which are women."

"Someone told me they are kept in the basement, like prisoners," he said and drank some coffee. There was trouble detecting his pulse, so I took my finger away.

Then he added, "I really don't care as long as I'm happy with the way things are. The maids are just decoration." He said that to throw me off. Since I couldn't feel his pulse, I couldn't prove anything. No matter what, I was determined to continue digging.

Later that day we went to Dr. Silverman's office to go over our case. I still wasn't pregnant. There were daily graphs of blood pressures and temperatures taken at different times. I really didn't care about that. All I wanted to know was the best time to make love. Dr. Silverman stood up to take a closer look at one of the graphics displayed on the screen. As I lifted my head to see what he was pointing to, I took in the details of his hand: veinless, without a single freckle. I realized that Dr. Silverman's white face was always expressionless. It looked like a paper mask that sometimes smiled or frowned. He had no wrinkles. No moles. No lines around his lips and mouth. He looked so young, but his voice sounded like it came from a deep cave, raspy and aged.

"Is something bothering you?" Dr. Silverman asked me, as Roberto turned toward me. I worried that they had discovered my suspicions about the woman with the scars. "Are you wondering about my life?"

I didn't answer.

"As I was finishing medical school, I wanted to manipulate memories to help victims of war." He lowered his head but looked up to the ceiling, as if trying to remember something. "We're all victims now." He clapped his hands hard, once. "Well, I never thought I'd end up restoring broken relationships. But the future of humanity lies in love. That's why we want you to have a lot of babies."

He went on about creating healthy relationships. "True love is only born out of having good memories, and we want you to love each other. Bad memories create scars. Although we can see scarred memories sometimes, many of them are hidden in the unconscious."

Dr. Silverman recounted some things I had said to him in previous sessions and explained that unconscious memories were causing my insecurities. *Is he thinking I might be jealous?* I wondered.

"If a bad emotional reaction is caused by an unconscious memory, we can capture it and alter it," he said.

Roberto said, "There's no need to torture ourselves. We can fix things and move on, regardless of what happened."

I almost yelled at both of them, but instead, focused on my breathing. I didn't want to end up in the giant machine that altered memories. I didn't want them to remove my most recent memories.

Roberto looked at Dr. Silverman, leaned forward a little in his chair, and placed his palm on his upper chest. "Doctor, I want to share something with you. Sometimes, even when I'm happy, I think about what my father said to me when I was a child. 'Don't cry. Never cry. Tears make you uglier than you already are. Just think of a way to survive. Always!' This memory creates pressure right here." He rubbed his chest. "When it comes up, I feel like I'm wearing a turtleneck sweater that is too tight for me. I want to have a sweater that fits."

And have a wife with scarred skin.

Doctor Silverman told Roberto that he would adjust his memories immediately.

I was too angry to stay. Even if Roberto noticed the scarred woman in those memory recordings, he would tell me that he didn't remember anything about it. But his sense of guilt could not be eliminated. Never. I still needed to prove that he'd wronged me.

Pretending to be tired, I left the office and went to the outdoor garden. At the building's exit, a maid was holding a basket filled with uniforms, sheets, and towels. She bowed and let me exit. The sunrays passing through the giant glass dome above prickled my skin as if I were being poked with millions of needles. I walked toward the dome's base, which was bordered by tall pine trees. Averting my eyes from the keep-away signs, I continued on. I wanted to peek at what was behind the trees, but the maid came after me. She blocked my way and pointed toward the clinic door, so I went back inside, where I saw the laundry basket the maid had left there. I took one of the uniforms, thinking of infiltrating the maids' quarters to discover that other woman.

That night, after making love with Roberto, I wanted to find the woman who'd slept with my husband. I had to do it that night. It couldn't wait until tomorrow because Dr. Silverman could mess with my memories, as he had done with Roberto. As Roberto snored on the bed, I put on the unitard that I'd stolen. My bracelet ID was impossible to remove, just as Dr. Silverman had said. It produced a barely noticeable bump under my sleeve edge. I hoped they wouldn't pay any attention to it and put on my head covering.

Why do we have so much implanted hair? Are the maids bald? Their head coverings seem so smooth. Maybe Roberto is attracted to bald women.

I headed to the basement. I saw a line of maids in front of a door with a plaque that read: Authorized Personnel Only. What amazed me was their silence. They didn't talk to each other. They looked like mannequins in a shopping window display. I joined the line, and the maid in front of me stretched her arms, yawning as if trying to reanimate her exhausted body. Everyone ignored her. I kept my head lowered and hoped that one of them would fold her sleeve back to reveal the scar I'd seen in the bathroom. At the same time, I stretched my sleeve down to make sure my bracelet ID It was covered. The maids didn't have IDs of any kind.

The door made a cracking sound as it slid open, allowing us to pass through. I was afraid that someone would check names, but we simply walked down another set of stairs. A strong odor of flesh, blood, and rotten mushy vegetables wafted up. I wanted to go back to Roberto, but the door behind me closed, so I went on.

A man was slumped against the bottom stairs, gasping. He had undone the top of his unitard, and his naked chest, completely burnt, looked like a scorched loaf of bread. I was surprised that the maid was a man. I passed him and walked into a room with six benches where the maids were sitting down to change their clothes. There were gym lockers along the walls. Except for the occasional sigh and the clicking, creaking, and thudding of the locker doors, there were no other sounds or words. Some of the maids had missing limbs, ears, or noses. And many had arms that looked like dry tree branches. There was a woman whose flat breasts looked like cracked windows with two holes occupying the place of the nipples. The room's odor gave me the sensation I was entering a giant belching mouth. I pressed my lips together to avoid vomiting. I realized not only that all of them had scars or lacerations but that they were also all bald. It was so shocking that I didn't want to think about the woman who'd slept with Roberto.

I felt dirty and wanted to return upstairs when, to my surprise, a man wearing a spacesuit and carrying his helmet under his arm approached the gasping man on the stairs.

"You can't go out any longer," he said to him.

"But . . ." the gasping man tried to object.

"Go rest. It's an order. I'm your supervisor."

The astronaut man turned and looked at me. One side of his face was missing a cheekbone, and it gave me the impression that I was looking at a reflection in a rippling pond. It seemed that he had supervisory authority as he said, "You, come with me. Grocery mission tonight." And he ordered me to wear a spacesuit that another maid gave me. As I was putting it on, he scrutinized me from head to toe.

"No prosthetics at all?" he asked as he squeezed my arms.

I shook my head, astonished at the question.

"Two eyes, two legs, two arms . . . good to carry groceries."

"Are your breasts natural?"

"Of course," I said, slightly offended. I put the astronaut helmet on before he could ask me about the bumps of hair covering my head.

"You look like one of those fertile women upstairs."

The word 'fertile' hit me like a rock. *That's what I am?* I felt like a brood cow.

He then led me through a labyrinth of corridors with shiny metal walls.

"Your first time outside the bubble?" he asked me.

I nodded, assuming he was referring to the clinic.

We arrived at a subterranean parking lot with rows of strange vehicles about the size of golf-carts. Each vehicle looked like a praying mantis and had six wheeled limbs, two larger ones in the front and shorter ones in the middle and back. A heavy sliding gate opened at that moment so another vehicle could exit.

"Hurry up; we need to catch up with them," the supervisor said, pointing to the gate. "They're part of my crew."

We ran to our vehicle as fast as we could with those heavy spacesuits and took the front seats. He looked at the dashboard clock and said, "It would be nicer to make morning trips, but the sun would cook us alive." As he continued turning on all the screens, he asked me, "Are you new here? What's your name?"

I thought about lying, but felt it was better to use my real name. "Victoria."

"It's a short trip for groceries. Any questions?"

"No, Mr. Supervisor," I said, even though it sounded awkward.

"You can call me Inuus. It means 'god of fertility.'" He glanced at the route on the computer screen. "I guess my mother wanted me to be someone who could have children. Can you imagine? I could be a patient of Dr. Silverman right now, trying to impregnate a beautiful wife with long hair." He looked at me again before starting the engine, stating, "They say the implanted hair helps them maintain the illusion." The gate clanged and slid open, revealing a second gate.

Inuus, pointing to his face, then said, "Not the best . . ." He shrugged. "Perfect arms and legs, though." He thumped his chest. "Strong."

The second gate opened, and we drove out. I expected darkness but was surprised by the brightness of a blinding light as the cart moved toward what seemed like a bonfire. I turned sideways to face Inuus. He probably thought I was flirting with him. He smiled.

The vehicle traveled up and down over dunes of metal scraps and collapsed buildings. There were fires everywhere. Further on, I saw a cascade of lava pouring out slabs of melting rocks and flinched when some of the viscous liquid splashed on our windshield. After another mile or so, there was a rainbow of flames, and the bright rays in the sky that made me feel as if I were inside a fireworks display. But the bumps, bounces and smacks of the vehicle made me worry that my body would be obliterated. I even felt slightly tipsy as I inhaled the chemical odor of the armor of my spacesuit.

The trip took no more than fifteen minutes. As soon as we arrived at a gated cave in a rocky mountain, Inuus asked me, "Do you know why this place is called Fossil Colony?"

I shook my head.

He drove inside, and the gate closed behind us. Long hallways were carved into the rock.

"Humans live here like those microbes that inhabit inside the rocks, don't they?" He chuckled. "Anyway, that's no reason. The President of this Colony explained that we all are just preserved remains of once living humans from the past" He parked the vehicle and sighed. "Very different from what my boss thinks of his Colony."

I gave him a questioning look, and he said, "Silverman, of course." And he went on, "Silverman's Colony still hopes for repopulating the earth with new and perfect offspring." I didn't understand what he was talking about, so I remained silent and nodded.

The vehicle before us had already arrived, and one of the team members held an infant car seat as he waited for us. "To survive and preserve life, we do not always play by the rules. Understood?"

I nodded.

Inuus stepped and took off his helmet as he approached him, and I followed, also taking off my helmet.

"He was born just a couple of hours ago. Dr. Silverman ordered me to discard him," said the man with the seat.

"You were supposed to inform me before departure." Inuus's eye flared. He pressed his lips and looked at the man and later at me. "Victoria. Our secret." He nodded, making me nod as well. He lifted his hand as if he were expecting an objection on my part and said, "I know it's against the rules. But those babies are humans, no matter what, even if they don't fit standards. I can't bring myself to just toss them like garbage. We bring them here where the Fossil people take care of them for the short time they live. We all can be fired if Silverman discovered that we're bringing their discarded babies to outside

Colonies." He paused. "We all." He looked me in the eye. "Can I trust you?"

I nodded.

"I knew you were one of ours." He smiled.

I tried to peek at the baby, and the man holding the baby said, "A gelatin baby."

My stomach revolted, and I closed my eyes, trying not to vomit. I didn't want to see that baby. I felt weak.

"I had thought to retire here one day, marry. I don't want to be a maid all my life." He smiled. "This Colony doesn't have conditions and high technology of Silverman's, but I don't have to hide under the unitard." Inuus went on talking, but his words dragged out like a tape recording in slow motion. Things around me began to look like a distorted oversized mirror. I fainted.

When I woke up, the first thing I noticed was the pain behind my head, a small bump that hurt. It was like a recently born creature, crying and calling for attention. A female wearing a white coat with facial skin like a melted candle slipped an ice pack under my head. I was lying naked on a hospital bed, covered by a bedsheet. I could have been at one of Dr. Silverman's clinic's rooms if it weren't for the rocks that formed the wall. A sink with a mirror in front of me made me think that this place had running water. Rays of light entered through three round windows that were really holes the size of my hand. An electric sliding door opened when it sensed someone right outside the room making an unbuckling noise. Two overhead electric bulbs, dangling from wires of different colors, illuminated my bed. Otherwise, the place was pretty murky.

"Did my husband have an affair with one of you?" I asked as I gripped the bedsheet tighter.

"I'm Doctor Eternity," she said, without asking for my name.

A minute later, Inuus came and stood by the bed.

"Where am I?" Fearing that Inuus's face would make me faint again, I focused my eyes on the mirror.

"The infirmary room. The Fossil doctors are taking care of you. We couldn't take you back to Silverman's." He took a small, soggy tomato from a bag he was holding and continued, "The people of Fossil managed to grow tomatoes, potatoes, mushrooms. They are real ones, not white powdered balls of protein bathed in holographic lights."

When I tried to touch the tomato, Dr. Eternity picked up my arm and showed my bracelet ID to Inuus. The skin on my arm was full of scars. I thought that something had happened when I fainted.

"Shit," said Inuus.

"Not only that," Dr. Eternity said as she uncovered my breasts, touching the halo around one nipple. "It's swollen."

Inuus rubbed his forehead, muttering.

Dr. Eternity took my arm again and said that she needed to take a blood test. After taking the sample, she stepped out to run the test. Inuus came closer and caressed the side of my head, causing a section of my implanted hair to fall on the pillow. "Of course, two legs, two arms, even two full eyes. You're one of those women from upstairs. I should have noticed that before bringing you outside. I'm a fool." He lifted my arm to show me my bracelet ID. "This bracelet causes everything you see in the clinic to look perfect. It projects a dream. A hologram. Holograms don't work here." He shrugged as if making an excuse.

"And she's pregnant," Dr. Eternity announced as the sliding door opened, making the unbuckling sound.

In my mind, all those people were of the same class, and one of them was the mistress. The news of the baby fueled my anger, and I couldn't hold it anymore. As Dr. Eternity approached my bed, I blurted my master plan, ending my whole story by saying, "I wanted to find that woman."

Dr. Eternity and Inuus kept quiet all the time while I was talking between sobs. And after a while, Dr. Eternity said, "To make the long story short, in Silverman's clinic, everything is covered with holograms, even your own body...sometimes the holograms fail, revealing what's really underneath. Of course, they don't coat every single spot." She sighed. "It appears that you're the woman that you were looking for. They recruited you. You consented. They erased your memories and covered your scars. And you think you live in a happy world with a beautiful body." She looked me in the eye, held up my arm, and then continued. Your entire body is like that."

I shook my head and looked to Inuus for some comfort, for even the slightest sign that this was some kind of game, but his eye—the eye on the good side—appeared vacant, as if he didn't want to acknowledge me.

I was trembling and sobbing, but Dr. Eternity lifted me into a sitting position to face the sink mirror. I closed my eyes. She laughed. "Now, you don't want to remember the person you are. You want to be blind, right? Let's play blind." She took my hand and rubbed it against my upper chest. My skin felt like tree bark, like when I'd touched Roberto's thigh. I cried harder, thinking that maybe that was why there weren't blind people anywhere in the clinic. The blind relied more on the tactile senses; in the clinic, we needed to see the things, the lie. *It couldn't* be true. I opened my eyes. The mirror revealed a splash of purple-reddish scars on my face. I reached toward my nose and rubbed it, hoping all of this would disappear in a minute. "This can't be true."

"That mirror is the real you."

I was dizzy. Things around me wobbled up and down, and a dark shadow grew from the bottom up. In a brushstroke, everything turned into a black pit.

When I woke up, Dr. Eternity was caressing my head.

"You fainted again," she said.

I told myself that this was all a dream, and I drank the water Dr. Eternity gave me. I told myself to remain calm until I woke up and found Roberto next to me. But it wasn't a dream.

Dr. Eternity told me that the previous governments preparing for nuclear war had developed atomic habitats that shield against the gamma rays and the inclemency of the hot weather. The shelter could host thousands who would live there for a couple of weeks. When the nuclear war destroyed the cities and transformed the earth into a kind of Mars, the governments and the UN fell out. Those shelters developed into forms of colonies for the survivors with their own governments. Fossil Colony is one of them, built underground under a rocky mountain as a form of protection, and Silverman's Clinic is another that was built above ground.

"We slowly grew and created some conditions for human survivorship. But we face a major problem. People didn't want to live. The memory editing program started as a way to cure people from their horrible experiences of a nuclear war. Here in Fossil, we don't believe in changing our memories. We believe in facing the past, no matter how painful it could be. Silverman, our closest neighbor, believes in creating an entire new past and history. So, he recruits people who voluntarily sign up to be part of his couples for—quote-unquote—treatment.

"I see. The clinic chooses people with a better possibility of survival," I said.

"Not at all," said Inuus. "Silverman chooses people that can successfully reproduce."

"They match people according to their DNA. Couples with the best chance of pregnancy are chosen."

"You lie," I yelled. I couldn't be a guinea pig, chosen because I could bear children.

"I myself tried to sign up for the program, but I was rejected," said Inuus. "Like many I'm also infertile." He gave me a sad smile, and I remembered the meaning of his name. "But they offered me to work for them."

"It's more than just to match fertile people. They tried to create the illusion of love. They make you believe that you're beautiful. Nobody falls in love with the monsters we are right now," said Eternity as she rolled her eyes.

"That's not true," said Inuus as he squeezed my arm.

"Come on!" Eternity threw her hands in a dismissive gesture. "Here in the Colony, we live as we are. We remember who we always have been: The horrible creatures who burnt the planet and left us like this. Of course, we want to recover hope. But the price we pay for living like this is that nobody wants to even have sex. For what, to populate the world with jellyfish?" She pretended to laugh in an exaggerated manner.

"Eternity, please. More respect for those babies." Inuus swallowed, and his eyes glittered.

"Sad that abortion is not possible in those cases," said Dr. Eternity as she placed her hand on my stomach.

"Forget about that," said Inuus, addressing me. "You don't need to come back to Silverman's." I shook my head, but he went on. "You have been exposed to radiation, and most likely, your baby wouldn't fit the genetic and physical standards. They are going to separate you from your child, and you won't even remember."

"Like the gelatin baby I saw earlier..." I mumbled.

"Don't get ideas in your head," Eternity scolded Inuus. "One thing is those babies who nobody wants, except us. Silverman's people turned a blind eye to it. Obviously. A fertile woman is another thing. And pregnant, which is worse."

Innus pleaded, "You have laws that protect her. And Fossil Colony never reports on a person looking for refugee status here."

"For those who escape. But she came here looking for her husband's mistress." Eternity laughed.

"I'm going to lose my job for nothing." Innus made a fist and tapped his forehead with eyes closed, but as he opened them, he said, "In two hours or so, they will find out that Victoria is missing...I just can take responsibility for it. Invent a story that...she is...my lover or something, and they may close any further investigation."

"That's your problem." Eternity jutted her chin. "I won't lie for her. She didn't escape that she never wanted to escape. That's what's needed to override her voluntary consent to sign up for that holographic paradise."

"You're risking the operation to save the rejected babies here," said Innus with a twisted smile. "They may launch a probe when you guys send her back."

"I. Do. Not. Care less. Now," Eternity mouthed. "We have a trade with them, and I don't care for those babies. I need medical supplies that Silverman provides to us."

Innus stooped up, rubbing his nape but as soon as he placed his look in the mirror, he mumbled, "I can do a cover-up in the meantime...and."

"You don't have to do anything," I yelled. I swallowed. "I just return right now." We barely had the time to be at Silverman's before they would notice I was missing. Inuus tried to convince me otherwise, explaining that maybe, the Fossil judges would allow me to stay as a refugee regardless of what Eternity would say. But I refused. Even though I knew that more radiation exposure was dangerous for my baby and that I lived in a place where my memories were implanted like my hair, I had Roberto. I wanted to convince him to escape with me. He was the only family I knew. I decided to return to Silverman's.

In bed next to Roberto that night after my return, I couldn't stop thinking about my conversation with Dr. Eternity. I couldn't stop thinking about the maids, those deformed creatures, their headquarters, the Fossil Colony, my trip with Inuus through a world made of fire, the gelatin baby, my pregnancy and my own scarred body. After we woke, I was silent as we got ready for our daily activities. Roberto kept asking me why I was acting so strange.

I couldn't talk as we went to have our breakfast. All I knew was that my toast, my eggs, the bacon on the dish, and the steaming coffee were all false. I was watching what the bracelet on my hand told me to see: a make-up world. I turned my head. My gaze got fixed on the maid sweeping the floor. Roberto held my hand, and I pulled it back. Roberto continued pressing me, asking me, "What's wrong?"

I stared at him, trying to see his face, his real face. I imagined him looking like Inuus, lacking a cheekbone and with the same purplish scars I had on my face. Could I love him like that? Could *he* love me without all of this...make-up?

I ran back to our room and locked the door. Should I tell Roberto about the other world out there? Or should I keep quiet and escape by myself? I thought about Doctor Eternity, Inuus, and the maids. At least they could be themselves. At least they had memories of their lives, the war, and what had gone wrong.

I heard someone knocking on the door, then heard Roberto say, "Victoria, Doctor Silverman is with me. Please open the door."

I knew exactly what that meant. They would take me to the machine and mess with my brain.

"Something is very wrong with you." Roberto said as he shook the door's lock in desperation.

"Victoria, whatever it is you're feeling right now, we can fix it." It was Dr. Silverman, the other liar.

I opened the door and looked at Dr. Silverman, saying, "I want to talk to my husband." I was about to slide my finger through my hair when I thought that my implanted hair, like an implanted memory, would fall off. If I stayed at the clinic, they would implant and erase memories again and again.

I grabbed Roberto by the wrist and yanked him into our room, and I closed the door for some privacy. I caressed his cheekbone. At first, I didn't feel anything. I even prayed that I couldn't feel any of his scars, but it wasn't like that. It was as if his skin was like an unpaved road. Then I realized that if they erased our memories, they also erased our suffering, even pain. How could we live like this without feeling pain? Are our children going to be able to sympathize with the others in pain and suffering, or would they be like me at the moment I saw the maid's scarred arm when I felt only disgust?

Roberto and I sat at the edge of the bed.

I kept silent for a moment until Dr. Silverman's steps faded away.

He caressed my cheek.

"What if this isn't the real me?" Confused, he didn't reply. I told him everything that happened the night before.

After a long silence, he said, "All I know is that I love the person I see."

"Roberto, this face isn't mine," I replied, pinching my cheek. "Everything is fake. It's a hologram that covers our scars. The true person we are inside. And sadly, now, we're breeding animals to preserve the human species. That's why the fertility treatment, the temporary amnesia. The falling hair. Everything."

"But you—we consented. You told me—"

"—I don't remember that. It's the same as I were being forced." I held Roberto by the shoulders, trying to look him in the eye. The phone that communicated the room with the reception area rang but we ignored it.

"Listen, the purpose of memory is to make you happy. I just want to remember as if I were watching a movie. A good movie. Without tragedies," he said as his cheeks turned rosy, that was something the holograms couldn't fake.

"No. I remember because I want to find the person, the real person inside me."

"I don't care about an atomic explosion forty, fifty, a hundred years ago. The now is what's important. Our family."

"Silverman is going to take away our baby," I yelled.

"But the baby isn't..." He caressed my earlobe and looked me in the eye. I moved away with anger, and he went on, "We need to erase all this. Doctor Silverman will take care of it." He stretched his arm to reach for the phone on the night table and pressed a button for the receptionist.

"Roberto, please, don't. . ." I said as I knelt on the bed, "Listen, we could escape and be ourselves, without. . ." I hesitated. "We could keep the memories we make every day."

The receptionist was already on the phone. "Escape?" Roberto repeated, without covering the phone's speaker. He held my chin. "We'll continue our treatment and then return to our dream home." He nodded while he spoke and looked for my assent.

I hugged my shoulders, rocking. I had to think about something, so I pleaded, "Listen, the people at Fossil can help us."

Roberto tossed the phone to the cradle and rushed to open the door. At that moment, the crew of nurses and doctors appeared in my bedroom. "Victoria, calm down," Doctor Silverman said.

"She wants to escape," Roberto mumbled as if he were embarrassed.

They grabbed me before I could jump out the window.

Now I'm lying in the scan machine, tied up on its rolling counter. The device that is going to erase my recent memories, the story that Eternity told me. The humming sound of the machine is a vacuum that will suck away all my desires to escape, to live up to my memories. A glaring light above my head makes me see halos around the light bowls. A human shadow appears outlined against the luminous circle behind. As the shadow leans toward me, I hear the call of my name, "Victoria." It's Roberto's voice. He places his hand on my shoulder, and I try to see his face, but I can't see his features. He's neither the scarred man nor the skin-perfect person covered by holograms. He's an unrecognizable shadow.

I close my eyes and turn my face away from him.

"Open your eyes." He repeats, in a whisper, "Open them. I want to see you like this forever."

I open my eyes as the machine rolls me to its mouth to eat the monster that I think I am.

NOT A CAT GUY

Cassandra O'Sullivan Sachar

Hey, man. Yeah, I'll have another. Got a minute? There's something I need to get off my chest if you're willing to listen. Thanks.

So I start dating this woman, you know? Not a girl but a real woman—hot, smart, total wife material. I'm in my 30s now, so I need to be done with those party girls. I want someone to do real grownup shit with, like go to my nephew's birthday party or dinner at the boss's house. A *woman*. And then I meet Amber through a friend of a friend, and I figure she could be the one.

Things were going great, slow, but whatever. She's been married before, but then her husband died like a year before I met her. That's how I got lucky and scooped her up, this chick totally out of my league—it turns out she was just putting herself back out there. Probably coulda gotten a better looking and more successful dude than me if she waited longer! She wasn't even on the apps yet.

Man, Amber's the real deal, like the first woman I dated who has opinions on stuff that matters, like politics and human rights and shit. She's just herself, you know? Unashamed to admit she enjoys reality TV and doesn't like watching sports or going to museums—she says she works all the time and is gonna do whatever she wants when it's *her* time. She says life's too short to do only what other people tell you.

We go through our honeymoon getting-to-know-you phase and hash out some shit. She says she's afraid to let her guard down around me after being epically wounded by her husband's death, and I make the mistake of saying I don't mind damaged goods, trying to keep it light, but that does *not* go over well, more like a fart at a funeral. At that point, I haven't been to her house yet, and that all comes out. We'd been together a couple of months by then, but we'd always gone to my place.

But we're solid, so we both apologize for what we said. Before I know it, she invites me over for this romantic dinner. And that's the night I meet *him*.

Amber mentioned she had a cat, and I'm not a cat guy, but I don't really care one way or the other. He's a rescue, an older kitten she adopted from the local shelter like six months before we met. No big deal to me since I'm not allergic; I'd just rather hang with a dog.

So, the night of, I put her address in my phone and drive like half an hour from my place to this fancy-ass neighborhood, a tree-lined cul-de-sac with brick and stone houses and a big sign announcing the swanky place, Thistle Grove. And I'm thinking that thistles are weeds, but still, it's the whole nine. And I'm feeling a little insecure if you wanna know the truth, with me living in a townhouse and the kind of restaurants I've been taking her to, but whatever. I'm here to check out my girlfriend's digs. I thought I was all suave buying her flowers—just a bouquet of daisies I picked up while getting some wine for dinner at the grocery store—and then I realize that both the flowers and wine are cheap and tacky, but I suck up my pride and head up the elaborate hardscaped walkway.

Amber swings the door open before I even reach it, wearing a low-cut black dress that I'm already imagining curled up on the floor of her no-doubt glamourous bedroom. She puts her arms around me even though mine are full and plants a soft, wet kiss on my lips, so I let go of my doubts and walk right on in.

Amber's giving me a tour of her place, and I'm feeling like a total schmuck when she pulls out this crystal vase for my pathetic flowers which look like crap in her tasteful foyer—probably foy-yay or whatever. And I'm wondering if I'm good enough for her, but then I know I'm not by the time we make it to the dining room where there's this huge-ass wooden table that I know isn't from Ikea or Target like pretty much all my furniture, and it's all laid out with dinner plates and real cloth napkins like it's a prom or something, and the smell is incredible like I died and went to heaven, but then that starts me thinking about her dead husband, the only reason I'm here in the first place.

Not gonna lie—I kinda peeked around for his picture when I was oohing and aahing over all the art and hardwood floors and shit, and I don't wanna be obvious, like how can I be jealous of a dead man when I'm the one who's gonna take Amber to bed that night? And I think I see a picture of her in a white dress with some dude, but it's not like a rule that she has to put photos of her dead husband away just 'cause her new boyfriend's over.

So I'm busy trying to act normal and appreciative of her effort, since I know Amber doesn't like to cook but she's still made this awesome fettucine alfredo and garlic bread anyway, and now I'm thinking I look like a clown slurping noodles off this fancy silverware, so I tell her about the (cheap) wine being from Chile and how my buddy Derek and his wife went on a trip there and no one ever heard from them again even though both sets of their parents went down there and launched a

GoFundMe. I even donated a couple hundred bucks. I miss that guy. And I find myself getting upset talking about it, wondering what happened, but then Amber's slender fingers are stroking my shoulder, making me feel better.

But that's when *he* comes sauntering in and jumps right up on the dining room table. Amber starts shooing him away and apologizing, and I'm kinda skeeved out that a cat's sitting right by the garlic bread after he might've just been messing around in his litter box, but I don't wanna be difficult when she's been so sweet and gone to all this trouble for me. I say it's fine, and the fucking cat stays there, his ass right on the table, and glares at me with these green eyes.

Amber's like, "This is my baby, Jacques." I hate when people call their pets their babies or their fur babies—it's a cat or a dog, not a baby. She gets into this whole thing about the darkness she felt after her husband died, but then she adopted the cat and he helped her find joy again.

Trying to be a good guy and thankful that this furball perked her up, I go ahead and give the little dude a pet. I figure that he helped get her ready to meet me, so I should be grateful. But the asshole swerves his head around like in "The Exorcist" and sinks his fangs into the meat of my hand. I don't wanna act like a wuss or harm him, but he does *not* let go, and it hurts like hell.

Amber starts freaking out and I'm trying not to scream or flail him around, but then Amber finally pulls him off me, and I'm dripping blood straight into my pasta. The cat runs out of the room after fixing me with this death stare.

Amber's all over it, running around with bandages and hydrogen peroxide, and I try to act chill but that fucker was surprisingly strong, and the punctures look and feel deep. Not to mention he has a mouth full of bacteria, so I'm picturing my hand swelling up with green pus and needing to get amputated.

But then I'm bandaged and cared for, and we're in the bedroom with our wine, and Amber feels so bad that she's giving me extra attention, rubbing my shoulders and taking off that dress and kissing my neck, and I kinda feel like my injury might have been worth it.

Afterward, we're nodding off in her big, magnificent bed. But then I jolt awake to this scratching sound at the door—really irritating, like fingernails on a chalkboard. In the dim light of the full moon, I see that fucker Jacques sneak into the bedroom. He jumps up on the bed and curls right up on Amber's chest like he didn't go all cat-Cujo on me! She's sound asleep by now and doesn't even register him, but I'm not messing around. I pull myself all the way to the edge of the king bed putting as much distance between us as possible, and I swear he smiles at me, but not a nice smile like he wants to be friends, more like he's laughing at me. But I somehow go back to sleep anyway, even though I'm a little nervous, to be honest.

When I wake up in the morning, before I even open my eyes, I'm aware of being watched and of a pressure on my chest. Sure enough, that bastard's sitting right on top of me, staring into my eyeballs like he's figuring out how to end me.

Amber's awake, too, smiling at us. "I think he's sorry," she says, giving him a pat.

This tremendous growl starts inside of the cat, and I'm waiting for him to lash out, waiting for new pain, for his claws to slash me across my face. My wounded hand stings in sympathy for whatever comes next.

"Relax, Jason, he's purring," she says, sensing my discomfort. "Give him a pet."

As much as I don't trust him, I don't like disappointing Amber, so I do, hoping Jacques doesn't want to upset her, either. And, I have to admit, that black fur is soft and silky under the fingers of my good hand, and he *is* kind of cute, but I won't forget what he did to me. He gives me this long, slow blink like he's trying to tell me something, but I don't speak cat, and Amber's gushing away. Before I know it, she's confessing her love for me and asking do I wanna move in.

We push the cat out of the way, him with a departing hiss directed at me even though I was just being nice to the little fella, and I swear that creep watches us the whole time we make love, but I look at Amber and remind myself how lucky I am. Amber leaves when we're done to take a shower, and soon Jacques jumps back on the bed, greeting me with another hiss and squinting his eyes like he wants to rip the skin off my face. I scowl back, but Amber's walking back into the bedroom with a towel on her head, and the cat slinks away.

Fast forward a month, and my townhouse is on the market and I'm moving my shit into Amber's place, giving away or taking all my chintzy furniture to Goodwill since it's not gonna fit in with her classy stuff. The cat's still screwing with me whenever Amber's not looking—hissing and swiping at me, throwing up in my shoes, I shit you not—but it's like we have a truce whenever Amber's around. He doesn't mess with me and I don't mess with him, not that I really do anyway. He's just a cat, but I glare at him and tell him to fuck off occasionally.

And then Amber goes on this business trip for a few days, and it's just the cat and me in her huge freaking house, and I'm in charge of feeding him and cleaning the litter box and stuff, which feels weird since the cat and I don't even get along, but she said she needs to be able to trust me to take care of him. I briefly consider hiring the teenage boy next door to do it, but I chicken out imagining Amber upset with me if she finds out.

So she's gone and I'm basically the cat's bitch now, feeding him this fancy gourmet food in his crystal dish like he's the king of cats, and Amber wants me to send a picture every day so she knows he's fine. I play along, trying to catch him sleeping so he doesn't hassle me, but we give each other a wide berth, more or less. He knows he needs me to give him food, and I know I need to be nice so Amber doesn't heave me to the curb.

But I swear he's still playing mind games with me. He wakes me up wailing at like 5 a.m. the first morning when he knows I'll be up for work in an hour anyway, and I go down to the living room to see what's the matter, like if he caught a mouse or something. He shuts up when I get there, so I turn on the light, not sure what to expect, and I see he's knocked down a picture frame—broke the glass and everything. I put on some shoes so I don't cut my feet, and I pick up the picture, and it's actually the wedding picture, Amber's wedding to her first husband, Greg. Call it my ego, but I never took a good look at it, didn't really want to act like he'd existed. But I'm forced to look now, my eyes still adjusting to the light, and that's when I see that this homeboy Greg has jet black hair and these light green eyes glowing out from the picture. And as I'm looking at this picture of the dead man who used to live here, this guy Amber loved before she even knew I existed, the cat starts making this weird noise, this chirping sound. I don't know what to make of it, so I replace the picture, clean up the glass, and go back to bed, but I can't sleep. I keep thinking about Greg, what was he like, and how if he'd lived I wouldn't be with Amber. And I feel kinda shitty for admitting this, but I'm glad he died.

Amber comes home the next day, and I have to tell her about Jacques knocking down and breaking the glass, and I feel weird since we never really talk about her ex.

"He's not my ex, he died," she reminds me, and I'm chastened and shamed, and I don't know if she thinks *I'm* the one who knocked it over instead of the cat, and maybe was he trying to get me in trouble?

But now that we're kinda talking about the not-ex-husband, it's like the ice is broken around the subject, and she brings him up more and more, like *Greg* used to do this and *Greg* liked that, and I'm feeling less and less adequate since this guy was handsome and basically a genius theology professor, not to mention loaded, like *old money* money, and I'm just an average-looking dude from Jersey who sells insurance. And she asks me to help her take some of his old stuff to Goodwill—he had all these books his family doesn't want and Amber doesn't want, either.

So I'm already living in the house this guy's money bought and shtupping his wife, so I figure I might as well go through his books to see if I can make sense of them. I'd like to think I'm not a total dumbass, but I can't make heads or tails of them, all these religious textbooks. But I see this one that looks interesting, like almost homemade, with this weird leather cover, no title or author on it, and the inside's all crinkly and old with faded writing that looks handwritten. No way it came from a regular bookstore or publisher. And—get this—it's all about reincarnation. And I know that fits in with his scholarship or whatever, but it's also about how you can *make* yourself come back after you die.

Most of it's over my head, and my hands feel tingly from touching it, like it's enchanted with black magic, so I get kinda spooked and make sure it's in the first box to head out of the house.

And that's when I think back to Greg's picture from their wedding, how he had black hair and green eyes, and I'm thinking about all this as I look up and see the fucking cat staring at me with this smug look on his face.

I know it's crazy, but it all starts coming together, and I think back to how long ago Greg died and when Amber got the cat, and how old the cat was when she got him and also how he hates me even though I've been feeding him and cleaning up after him, so I stare him right in the face and ask him if he's Greg.

I'm half expecting him to open his mouth and talk to me, but he just lifts up his leg and starts cleaning himself, which I'm pretty sure means *fuck you* in cat language.

So I start doing some deep diving on the internet, looking up stuff about Greg and how he died, which I never asked Amber about 'cause I wanted to respect her privacy and what she shared with her husband, but if the husband's actually Jacques then I need to be able to protect myself. I find out he had leukemia, but I also find this picture of him about a year before he died at this temple in India somewhere, and I think that's where he got that book and plotted coming back as Jacques.

And Jacques knows I'm on to him, and I start wondering what he's going to do to me, if he's going to try to get rid of me somehow, so I start acting extra careful, making sure he can't get me into trouble somehow. But he's smart—you need to be in school forever to get a PhD, you know? And I don't know how much he retained from his life as a man, but Jacques definitely has my number by this time.

Then I have this crazy dream one night—at least I think it's a dream. Jacques is speaking to me in what I know is Greg's voice since I found some clips of him online from academic conferences where he gave presentations, and he's telling me that Amber is his and he's gonna find a way to get rid of me, and I know this shouldn't be scary since it's more like a Disney movie with a fucking talking cat, but I wake up in a cold sweat with my heart pounding out of my chest. And the cat's staring at me like it all really happened, and maybe it did.

I don't say anything to Amber through any of this, just keep acting like everything's fine and she has a perfectly normal asshole of a cat versus a dead husband reincarnated as a cat. I know I'd sound crazy, and she wouldn't like that I'm snooping around trying to find things out about Greg and looking at all his articles he wrote and listening to some of his recorded lectures and stuff.

But then one day I'm chilling watching the game and she comes home from work, and, before she even gives me a kiss, she's calling for her precious little Jacques, so I go back to watching TV. I don't even realize how much time has passed until she's standing in front of me screaming and crying, and I'm just like, "What?"

She says I left the back door open and Jacques is gone, like, out of the house gone, and that he could be lying dead on the side of the road somewhere because he's not an outside cat and doesn't know how crossing the street works. And part of me thinks how peaceful it would be without Jacques, but I know not to say that just like I know I didn't leave the door open. I know *he* did it to frame me.

Three days. Three days Amber's sobbing every night, missing him, giving me the cold shoulder. I'm trying to do all the good boyfriend stuff—put up flyers, you know, contact rescue centers. Somebody calls us and we go to meet them, but it's some other black cat. I would've been happy to take any other cat home and just pretend it's Jacques, so I even try to make her think it's him, but she gets all pissed off like how could I possible think this scraggly thing is her sweet baby, and I'm hoping this dude isn't also a man reincarnated, 'cause it's pretty harsh to say that about him when he's just a poor stray cat with no one to love him.

So Jacques is still gone, and I try to cheer Amber up, bring her Starbucks and stuff, give her a foot massage, the whole nine, but she's livid with me even though I'm innocent. And we're sitting in the living room, me finally getting pissed off that she's blaming me, her crying and snotting everywhere, and then we hear this scratch at the door.

So I get up to open the door, and there's that cocky little bastard, looking roughed up and dirty, and he just runs into the house and launches himself onto her lap.

It's this big tearful reunion between them, so I go over thinking I'll get back into Amber's good graces. I go to pet Jacques and he lunges at me, scratching my hand.

But Amber doesn't faun all over me like when Jacques bit me that first time I came over. She's all like, "I knew it. I knew you didn't like him! I knew you let him out!" She's up on her feet, her face all scrunched up and red, tears and mucus streaking her face, shouting, cursing at me, and I'm pretty much in shock since I still didn't even do anything to the damn cat, but I look over and see the cat laughing at me.

I try to reason with her, try to make her see it was Jacques trying to come between us, and I spill the beans about Greg and how he found out how to come back to her. She looks at me like I'm a lunatic, so I give her all my proof, and she goes all still before telling me we're done.

She only gives me to the end of that week to move out. So that's that, and Jacques/Greg gets the girl.

Yeah, yeah, I know you have other customers, but I'm your best one, right? And can I get one more beer, man? Just trying to take the edge off before I head home to my shitty new apartment where I'm sleeping on a futon since I sold my place and got rid of my furniture. Thanks, man. That fucking cat.

AUTUMNAL EQUINOX REDUX

Will Lennon

Bill Bennet weighs a brick in his hands, pondering how best to smash the front windshield of his 1979 Pontiac Firebird Trans Am.

The brick is just something he picked up in a vacant lot. It's old and worn, losing its shape. Maybe, he thinks, running his thumb across its rough surface, he should find a new one, with corners sharp enough to cut. Gravel crunches beneath his boots as he paces.

He decides to go with what he has, for now. Closing his eyes, he heaves the brick at the laminated glass, aiming for the center left. There's a crunch. The impact leaves rings of breakage radiating out across the windshield.

It's all wrong.

He sighs, picks up the brick and sets it aside. He gets behind the wheel and drives past two different auto repair shops to get to one where they don't ask questions. A replacement windshield costs him $300.

The next morning, Bill's clock radio chirps. He doesn't get up at first. He wants to lay there on his futon, with plastic shutters drawn against the sun all day. But instead he rolls to sitting and twists the little plastic wand by the window. The shutters clack sideways. Yellow bars of light bisect his bedroom wall, fully overtaken by bits of notebook paper, crisscrossed with lengths of string and wire, all held together with clear tape. All the strings and wires lead to a worn out black air freshener, shaped like a pine tree. Bill sits Indian-style and studies the tree. His creature comforts (a half-empty pack of cigarettes, loose joints, beat up paperbacks, spiral ring notebooks) are scattered on the floor.

Minutes later he pulls on his dirty jeans and an Against Me! t-shirt he's had since high school. In the kitchen, he watches the instant coffee machine piddle watery-brown into the pot. His roommate says hi on her way out.

"You're up early," she says, hovering by the door. "Morning shift?" She doesn't really want to talk. She's freshly showered, wearing her toothpaste-blue nurse's uniform, white tennis shoes and a laminated name tag: Cora Gutierrez. Cora is always working, it seems. There's a nurse-shortage, so she's always driving way out of town to take on time-and-a-half shifts.

Bill shakes his head.

"I quit," he says.

"Oh?" she says. "Got something else lined up?"

"Nah. I just want to focus on driving," he says, pouring the coffee into his thermos. The thermos is ancient and dented, but it's covered in stickers for long-gone bands that he can't replace, so he keeps it.

Outside, he grinds the base of the thermos into the gravel, so it'll stand upright. He palms a new, store-bought brick, smooth and red. He doesn't want to throw another brick at his car. He loves this car. He loves the roar of its 455 cubic inch V8 engine, he loves the twin chrome exhaust pipes, the cruel glint of the honeycomb wheel. He loves how the black paint job makes it shimmer in the sun like an obsidian insect and contrasts with the art on the hood.

Instead of the traditional "screaming chicken" decal seen on the hoods of most '79 'birds, his has a portrait of a woman. From a distance, she's often mistaken for an L.A. classic, the Virgen de Guadalupe, surrounded by roses and radiating light. Close up, she's more demon than saint.

Unlike the Virgin, this woman has her back to the viewer. She is slipping out of a red and black kimono, peering over her shoulder. A smile plays across her lips.

The kimono is covered in intricate designs, rich blacks and reds against her white skin. Lining the kimono's hem are whirlpools of fire. There are people caught in their currents, some with their eyes sewn shut, some with elaborate torture devices clamped to their arms and legs, some covered in insects. All are screaming. In the sky above them, a laughing ogre reads from a scroll, its pink tongue lolling. A red sun ripples in the sky above, distorted by folds in the kimono's fabric. On the sleeves, angels (or maybe Buddhas?) with white beards and dark robes look on with somber expressions, clutching wooden prayer beads.

Bill has no idea who made the decal. It was on the Firebird when he found it. But he loves it. It's so heavy metal.

But the Firebird is 44 years old. The guys at the shop tell him it's not long for this world. If he wants to keep it on the road, he'll have to make repairs so intensive that it will turn into a Ship of Theseus. That's why, if he's ever going to give this a real shot, he has to do it now.

He throws the new brick.

The second the brick leaves his hand he knows it's not right. The old brick wasn't the problem. It was something more subtle. The angle, the arc, the velocity, or some configuration of the three. Impact confirms. This brick actually penetrates the windshield, punching out a brick-shaped section of glass and then getting stuck. Most of the surrounding windshield is undamaged. It looks like the brick just sank into the glass, the same way it would have pushed into something gelatinous.

The bit of glass displaced by the brick is puddled in the seat. He grabs his old snow brush from the trunk and sweeps the glass. It tinkles to the gravel like sharp rain. It is the first time he has used the brush since Michigan, he realizes. The plastic handle feels familiar and comforting in his hand.

Not daring to yank it out, he drives to the shop with the brick suspended in windshield-purgatory.

That night, in bed, Bill waits for morning. When he closes his eyes, he can see the perfect shatterpath. Every inch is stored in his memory. Through it, he has seen a hundred dark highways.

He wonders if it would be worth trying to use a glass-cutter to carve the shape into the car himself. Tricks like that rarely work. It is more important that the breakage be caused by a brick than it is to get the exact shape right, but the shape does matter.

He has rules like this written in a blue spiral-ring notebook on his table. There are dozens of entries, scrawled over the course of ten years. To most people, any given page would read like gibberish.

Put a Marb Red behind your ear and speed on I-710 S while listening to a scratched Shelshag CD. Equals drive to Fourth of July picnic, Holland, Michigan, 2009.

Wear too-tight boxers and suck on a cough drop. Accelerate to thirty miles per hour on mountain road between 2 and 3 a.m. Equals drive home from Brick Mower show, Pyramid Scheme, Grand Rapids, 2012.

NEVER LEAVE THE CAR WHEN NIGHT DRIVING.

Bill rolls out of bed and picks up the notebook, twisting it into a tube and shoving it into his back pocket, even though he doesn't need it. He has the trigger-shift he's going to use tonight memorized. He pulls on his worn leather jacket.

On the freeway, he merges into the slashing evening traffic. The city is saturated in a fog of light. He drives until the sky turns clear and black. With the windows rolled down, the air tastes like trees and soil and smooth stones blasted clean by rain.

He tunes the radio to a station that plays old country. Waylan Jennings, Patsy Cline, Johnny Cash. He needs radio for this drive. Streaming the music, or even playing a CD or tape, doesn't work. That's part of the reason L.A. is good for night driving. Good radio.

He only needs two tokens for this trigger-shift. The first is that the station has to play a Johnny Cash song, and it has to be a Johnny song from before the Rick Rubin sessions in 1994. With songs from '94 and after, the trigger still works, but it's unpredictable. You never know where it will send you. Songs from the American Recordings album shifted Bill into all kinds of weird drives that he's never been able to access again. Once that album got him stuck in some city he didn't recognize. It looked like New York, but there were no street signs or names on the storefronts. The whole city was abandoned, and a reddish glow, like brake lights, seeped up from the storm drains. He drove around for hours and then suddenly found himself in Glendale.

The second token is a pair of sunglasses with a little Michigan flag decal on the side. The lenses are worn and scratched from years of alcohol induced accidents and carelessness, but he could never replace them. He puts the sunglasses on and tunes the radio to the country station. It's his lucky night. Almost immediately, Johnny's Orange Blossom Special plays. He feels the jolt.

The body of the Firebird is a smooth black brick, passing through a glass windshield without a crack or ripple. He knows this drive well. If he wrinkles up his brain a certain way, he can see around its corners, experience the end and beginning simultaneously.

Carrie Quinn's hair was black. Not brown. Black as a crime against physics, the sort of black that sucked in light and framed her face in an event horizon, an anti-halo. Her skin was white and soft, except for a couple of pink flecks on her cheeks that she scrubbed with Stridex pads before bed. She wore a Gaslight Anthem t-shirt and black jeans. Her boots were sitting empty at the base of the passenger's seat where she was curled up, sleeping on the morning after her 21st birthday.

The rhythm of her breath changed. She stirred and cracked her eyes open. They were the color of emeralds, flecked with gold.

"How much longer?" she asked.

"We're almost there," he said.

Old farmhouses zipped by. The sky, overcast and cloudy, rumbled. The trees are lush and green.

Bill stops himself. Were. The trees *were* lush and green. This isn't the seed-drive. That happened in 2015, in Michigan. Rule number one of night driving: never fully lose track of the now. Keep your eyes on the road. He wasn't ready to break that rule.

Carrie wrapped her arms backwards around the headrest and clamped left hand around her right wrist. She yawned flamboyantly, thrusting her hips forward and arching her back. The waistband of her shorts slipped, and Bill could see the little cartoon cherries printed on the waistband of her underwear. She has a thing for clothes with fruits and desserts printed on them.

Had a thing. Past tense. He doesn't know whether Carrie still wears underwear with cherries on them. He doesn't even know if Carrie is still alive. Maybe she has children and lives in a house. Maybe her hair isn't black anymore.

The yawn dissipated and Carrie folded her legs. He rested his right hand on her knee. A song called Sun Bleed by the band NE-HI played on the stereo.

In slow motion, she rolled her head to the side, locked her eyes with his. Her lips separated.

"I have to pee," she said.

Bill swung the Firebird down the next exit ramp and found a truck stop, a massive one with movie halls and public showers alongside its convenience stores and gas pumps.

"Be right back," she said, hopping out. Bill nodded and fiddled with the music. He had one of those adapters that let you play music from your iPod through an old tape deck. In a few minutes, Carrie bounded out of the truck stop and Bill opened the driver's side door.

"I got you these," she said, tossing a black pair of sunglasses into his lap. He picked them up and examined them. They were truck-stop sunglasses alright. "Cheapies." They had a decal of the Michigan flag on the side.

"You've been squinting," she remarked. "Bad for your eyes." She was always on him for stuff like that. Spraying him down with aerosol sunscreen in summer, stuffing his gloves with warming pads in winter. At 23, he was a come-what-may type of guy. At 21, she was a Green Beret, ready for any situation, her backpack crammed with whatever you need to spend a day at the beach or climb Mount Everest.

He unfolded the sunglasses.

"You sure I don't look stupid?" he asked, putting them on.

The sunglasses sat crooked. She reached to adjust them, and he grabbed her by the arm and pulled her onto his lap. They kissed, and his cerebral cortex exploded. Images flashed. Together at school, their hands laced. Carrie in his bed, sharing her pale body in the dark. Carrie in the passenger seat of the Firebird, the night they found it on the first day of fall. He cups her face. Her cheek feels small and soft in his hand. He will find a way to stay in this moment forever if it kills him.

Then an image of something that never happened: the two of them leaving Michigan, heading east together, the Firebird crammed with everything they owned.

Two futures sit side-by-side. L.A. and New York. They clash. The sweetness of New York leeches into L.A., crystalizing like sugar. His life aches like a rotten tooth. The darkness of L.A. bleeds into New York. Bill and Carrie feel something dark accumulating in the sky. The kiss turns bitter.

Their lips separated. As Carrie collapsed back into her seat, smiling with her eyes averted, Bill is pulled into darkness.

The taste of her lip balm dissipates as his eyes adjust. He is in California, in the parking lot of a suburban Target. There's another car in the lot, a group of Hispanic teens, two boys and two girls. They're laughing at the strange man in the beat-up old Firebird, wearing an oxblood-red leather jacket in summer and sunglasses at midnight.

He still isn't sure what happens to him when he night drives, but whatever it is must have looked funny to them. That's why they're laughing. One of the teens comes over and raps on the driver's side window. He's holding a 7-Eleven slushie. The others are barely containing their laughter.

"Hey man," he says. "Nice car." Bill puts the car in gear and peels out, and the teen has to stagger back to keep from getting sideswiped. They swear at him in Spanish as he speeds out of the parking lot. The slushie explodes against the Firebird's rear bumper.

"I'm sorry," he mutters, pulling onto the highway. "I'm sorry, I just need to drive."

He drives all night. The road's segmented center lines whip past in staccato. He wants to turn them into a blur, into a solid strip.

Next morning, the clock radio chirps like an insect. 6 a.m. Bill doesn't want to get up.

He doesn't update the chart on the wall or add anything to the notebook. There is nothing new to report. He has been trigger-shifting to that drive for years. Some days it's his only escape. He has spent weeks and months on that stretch of rural Michigan road. He lives in fear of losing it. He's lost drives before.

Once there was a coffee shop in Glassell Park called Division 3. D3 sold vanilla lattes that tasted just like the ones sold at Lemonjello's coffee, in Holland, Michigan. They even came in the same cheap, brown paper cup. If Bill bought one of those D3 coffees around 9:30 in the morning (it had to be after 9 and before 10, but 9:30 was the most reliable time) and then drove on a clear day wearing a certain green windbreaker and with a day-old, half-empty can of Orange Crush open in the back seat cupholder, he could night drive to the morning his dad taught him to drive the Firebird. It was just before the divorce, before things got weird.

Then came the overdose. And the looney bin. And the interviews with detectives and lawyers and Mental Health Professionals. And then, soon after, Bill started night driving. And it all started fading away. Carrie was still around then. "My family is fucked up too," she would say. It was true. Her dad was a withdrawn, right wing lunatic. Her mom was a meltdown-machine who chased her around with a leather belt. She understood everything but the night driving.

He can't get back to that drive with his dad anymore. The coffee shop closed down during the pandemic. He tried to find a similar place with similar cups and similar drinks. He tried ordering the exact cups from a restaurant supply store and recreating the drink at home. He even tried driving back to Michigan, just to sit in LJ's like he and Carrie used to. He figured that maybe he didn't need to night drive. Maybe sitting alone in that room where they used to come in from the cold and snow to warm up and play checkers and get into fights and break up and drink lattes from cheap, brown paper cups would be enough.

But he couldn't make it to Michigan driving the Firebird anymore. There were too many hidden triggers along the highways connecting Los Angeles to Lemonjellos, and the more he drove, the more easily he shifted. Getting to California's eastern border took him 4 hours in real time. But it felt like days. He turned back and went home.

At least in L.A. he knows where all the triggers are. He can track them with notebooks and charts. Usually at least. He suspects some drives have a quantum nature. Observing them, or focusing on them, can cause them to skitter away or blink out of existence, make you forget they were ever there.

He slips on a dirty Bad Religion t-shirt and smokes a Parliament. He wants to get this next disappointment over with.

"Don't overthink it," he mutters to himself. He stares at the Firebird, studying the expression of the woman on the hood. Doing his best to feel as serene as she looks, he lowers his sunglasses over his eyes and flicks the cigarette by the filter with the tip of his tongue so that it rolls to the corner of his lips. He turns away from the car and walks over to where the beat up old brick is nestled into the gravel. He picks it up and weighs it in his hand. He hears Cora's keys jingle.

"Good morning," she says, her key sliding out of the side-door lock. He exhales.

He tosses the brick over his shoulder. Cora stares as the brick bashes a shatterpath into the windshield. Bill looks over his shoulder. He smiles.

"Good morning," he says.

Bill spends the day out on the road, driving, admiring the shatter path. It's perfect. He can hardly believe it.

Tonight he will attempt something new: trigger shifting in a drive. That is, a night drive within a night drive. By going two layers deep, he hopes to bypass a blown tunnel, to access a gone-away-drive.

Then, he means to leave the Firebird and stay forever.

It had been a simple drive to trigger, back when he had the tokens he needed. He would hang a black pine tree shaped air freshener from his mirror. It had to be a certain scent, "Nightfire," that smelled like campfire and old leather. Then it was just a matter of driving fast, in top gear, and breaking 80 miles per hour while breathing in the Nightfire. But he hadn't been able to do it in years.

Back then, he didn't take trigger-shift tokens as seriously as he should have. When the first Nightfire air freshener wore out, he went out and bought a new one. He should have bought the entire box. He should have asked if they had a palette in the back and if he could swing by and pick it up in a U-Haul. It didn't occur to him that he might arrive in a future when they would be discontinued. But they were, so when that second Nightfire lost its scent, the tunnel was blown.

He was living in L.A. by the time he realized what he had done. He must have driven to every gas station in town. They offered him every other scent. Pina Colada. Black Ice. Lavender. Supernova. No good. He needed Nightfire. *Needs* it. And the last place he can remember seeing it was on a spinner rack by the checkout of a gas station outside of Las Vegas in 2018. So that's where and when he needs to go. And the only way he knows how to shift back there is with a broken windshield.

It's almost time. Bill has to be exhausted to make this trigger work. He has to drive for hours, to the point where he's pinching himself to stay awake. The skies are choked with smog. Yellow in the day, deep red at night. They're turning red now. The valley roils beneath him, like a cauldron full of something thick and shimmering. He looks out onto a fractured highway. The zero-line rushes up. There's a jolt.

They were on the outskirts of Las Vegas, far from the lights of Fremont and the strip, zipping past strip malls and Starbucks in the dark. The sky was full of stars.

"I'm sorry," said Val, her voice hoarse.

She was wearing all black. Black jacket, black jeans, black boots, up on the dashboard. She even had her hair dyed black, though she had missed some spots. She wore it long in the back, blunt in the front. The blacks of her green eyes were dilated in the dark. The whites were pink from crying.

Bill cleared his throat and looked back out at the road. But that just meant looking at the massive smash-mark on his windshield. Val cracked the passenger window and took a puff from one of her long, fragrant Euro-cigs.

"Can't I have some forgiveness?" she pleaded. But forgiveness wasn't what she wanted. She wanted an apology of her own.

Her accent was thicker than he remembered it. The first time he ever heard her speak was when he wandered up to her at a festival and asked who she was there to see. "Angel Olsen," she said. "Ahhn-Jeehl Ohl-Sohn."

"It would be easier to believe you were sincere if you weren't already smoking in my car again," he said quietly. She glared at him.

"What is this car to you?" she said. "You think you can't tell me? After I've given my whole heart to you?"

Bill gripped the steering wheel. He turned up the stereo. He had upgraded and gotten a new system installed, so he could play MP3s via a USB port. This was when he was more cavalier about making modifications to the Firebird. Nowadays he wouldn't dream of doing something like this.

"It's my car," he said. "It's not so complicated. What, your other boyfriends didn't mind when you bashed their windshields with bricks?"

"There are no 'other boyfriends,'" she spat. "And you know I know it's more than that. You're lying. Obfuscating. Changing the subject."

"I'm not changing the subject," he said.

"I gave myself to you," she repeated. "Bled for you, straight from my heart." She started to cry.

"Maybe it really isn't about the car. Maybe you aren't out driving in the desert every night. Maybe you're going to see some other girl. Maybe this is how you trade us off."

"Val," he sighed. "I told you, I just drive. It clears my head."

"All night? Every night? It's half mad what you do. You don't sleep. Just once I want to sleep next to you, all night."

"I sleep," he muttered. "I sleep. You just miss it. You miss me when I come in."

"Lying," she said again

He sighed. He hated being here. Hates. But he is just passing through.

Bill steeled himself and cranked the steering wheel right. Val turned to him, her eyes narrowed. For a moment Bill could have sworn that she somehow knew they were breaking script. But probably she was just wondering why they were pulling into a gas station with a full tank.

"What's wrong?" she asked.

"Nothing," he said. "I just need a couple of things. Could you get me a Diet Coke? And a new air freshener?" She stared at him.

"Why don't you go get it?" she asked incredulously. "I'm smoking."

"Exactly. You're smoking up my car, so I need an air freshener. The one that looks like a little tree. The scent I like is called Nightfire. Please?"

"My God," she muttered. She flicked her cigarette.

"Nightfire," he said as she stalked around the hood. She shot him a filthy look over her shoulder and jammed her hands into her jacket pockets. Bill drummed his fingers on the steering wheel.

By now they were supposed to be getting onto the highway and driving through the night to San Francisco. They were supposed to hike up through Redwoods to see a view of the Pacific Ocean and find nothing but mist. Bill was supposed to apologize.

Val emerged from the gas station. She got back into the car and tossed a plastic bag onto the center console. She put her boots back up on the dashboard. Trying to look calm, Bill fished around the bag. There it was. His hand shook as he hung it around the rearview mirror.

"Are you alright?" Val asked.

"It's fine," he said, starting the Firebird and throwing it into drive. Val stared at him as he accelerated onto the highway. She started crying, softly. Bill turned up the Hot Chip song playing on the stereo (Over and Over) so that the car was filled with sound. The road was open. He drove fast. He tried to focus on Nightfire, vibrating with the Firebird's engine, and on the beat of the song, thrumming against his heartbeat.

The speedometer's needle surged to the right. The Firebird growled. Bill kept his eyes on the road. He was so close.

"I don't want to listen to this anymore," Val said. She picked up the iPod.

"Hey," Bill said. "Hang on-"

Too late. Val changed the song to "Intern" by Angel Olsen. He looked in a panic at Nightfire, at the speedometer. It was too late to change course. He was shifting into the wrong drive. Bill felt a jolt.

Bill was drenched in cold sweat. The afternoon sky was blue, and he was weaving through traffic, but he wasn't on the highway. Everywhere around him people laid on their horns as he blasted through lights and stop signs.

He didn't want to look in the back seat, but he knew what was back there. He could picture it. Skin bleached powder-white. Nose caked clown-red. Chest shuddering, not moving regularly, with the rhythms of breathing, but twitching, like a bird on the patio after slamming against a clean window. He had gotten blood and powder all over his hands and chest when he loaded her into the backseat. Her blood, his powder. The stereo was still on, playing "Angels" by The xx.

"Hang on," he muttered. "Hang on, hang on." She made a sound that was more like drowning than breathing.

He took a hard right and jumped a curb into the Hospital parking lot. At the emergency room entrance, he used the parking brake to skid to an ugly stop.

Bill spun out of the front seat and ran to the back driver's side door. He hoisted her up in his arms. She was limp. That was good, he remembered. Limp was better than stiff. He ran for the automatic doors, her head bobbing to the side, blood dribbling onto the concrete. Two men in scrubs appeared as the doors slid open.

"Grab a MAX cart," one said, taking her.

"Her name's Valentine. Valentine Corbyn-Leroux," Bill sputtered. "She's Canadian. She's... She's allergic to shrimp. I think."

In seconds, Val was strapped in onto a cart, surrounded by doctors, being wheeled down the hall. He stood by the door, blood congealing into a tacky brown crust between his fingers. The Firebird idled on the other side of the glass doors, waiting for him.

He looks to the Firebird. Things tend to get weird when he leaves the car. Of course, the breaking of that very rule is the lynchpin of his plan. The problem is that this is the exact wrong drive to execute it. But this is also his chance to find out what happened to Val.

When he got to the emergency room, they were wheeling her down a hallway, out of site. He tried to go after her, but a nurse blocked his path.

"Sir," she said, as he tried to angle his way around there. "Sir, you can't go back there. *Sir!*"

Bill managed to spin around the nurse and bump directly into a security guard. A beefy hand pressed against his chest.

"I'm going back," Bill seethed. "You have no idea what I'm risking by being here."

The security guard shoved him.

"You are the last person she needs to see right now," he said flatly. "Trust me. I deal with guys like you all the time."

"Fuck off," Bill hissed. "Fuck you. You're a *figment*. You're an electrical impulse in my brain. All of you! I'm from the year 2024, you shadows! I'm flesh and blood! You disappear when I'm not looking!"

The security guard said something into his walkie-talkie. He replaced it on his belt holster with a static hiss.

"Have a seat," the security guard said.

"Fuck you!" Bill said. "I can... I can..."

He could what? Night drives didn't change the future, he knew that. That meant they weren't real. They were in his mind. So shouldn't he be able to suck the oxygen out of their lungs? Rush all the blood in their bodies up their necks and make their heads pop like whiteheads? He heard footsteps behind him. Reinforcements. Bill spun on his heel and extended his hand, palm out, willing the laws of physics to bend to his will. Two security guards froze.

They stared at his outstretched hand. They glanced at each other.

Bill felt a sharp crack against the side of his head. Stars flashed before his eyes followed by a burst of pain. The floor rushed up. In the moment before a red fog covered his eyes, he saw the security guards and nurse staring down at him. The one who had stopped him from following Val into the back room folded up a collapsible baton.

"Kid thinks he's fuckin' Magneto," he said.

In the fog, their eyes glowed like yellow diodes. Blood poured into his nose and mouth. It was hard to breath.

Bill sucks in.

Sucked? No, sucks. He's back in the Firebird, and the road is whipping past, but it's the wrong road again. No, not just the wrong road. The wrong way. He has jumped the divider. The yellow lights are oncoming traffic. There's a terrible cacophony as everyone lays on their horns at once.

"No," he gasps. "No, no-" he cranks the steering wheel to the right and jumps the divider again, just in time to avoid being slammed by three lanes of highway traffic. But now he has a new problem. He is crashing into the left-most lane, which is fully occupied at the moment, so to rejoin traffic he's going to have to shove someone else to the right. The Firebird is sturdy. It easily shoves a Toyota Camry to the side to make room for itself. But then that Toyota Camry is skidding horizontally across the freeway, trying to regain traction, knocking other cars out of their lanes. Way on the other side of the road he sees a Chevy Malibu go into a ditch.

He has to get out of here, now. He accelerates and whips out in front of the mess, then swings across three lanes to shoot out the next exit. He prays the chaos is thick enough for no one to have read his license plate number.

He finds a 24-hour parking garage and pays half the remaining contents of his checking account to pull in. He finds a spot and shuts off the engine. In the distance, he hears sirens. It's probably safe to assume someone is looking for him. He gropes for the notebook and pen in the back seat. He writes:

"-East Las Vegas Exxon DOES have Nightfire.

-Val will retrieve. Minimize engagement.

-DO NOT let her change music. AO Intern is a token."

He closes the notebook and slumps down. Within a few minutes, he is asleep.

A few hours later, the sirens go quiet. Bill drives home on city streets, avoiding the highway. He lets himself into the house quietly, to avoid waking Cora, although she'll be up soon anyway.

He doesn't really feel like sleeping, so he takes a shower. It's his first in a while. He hasn't been doing his morning routine since he quit his job as a forklift jockey at the Van Nuys Home Depot. The steaming water burns four days of grunge off his body. Brown sludge swirls down the drain. He's out of shampoo, so he washes his hair with a bar of soap. He squirts some of Cora's toothpaste onto an underused brush and scrubs the top layer of scum off his teeth. After he is clean, he sits down in the base of the tub. Steam rises from his skin like smoke.

Hours later, Bill stirs as the tangerine glow of dusk seeps through the pink membranes of his eyelids. He must have forgotten to set his alarm and slept all day. He rolls to sit.

He drives down by the beach and some teenagers in a souped-up Toyota Supra challenge him to race. He takes them up on it and wins. It feels good, but he's just killing time.

He drives up to the mountains, examining the shatterpath. It still looks good. The sky is turning red. It's time to try again.

Val emerged from the gas station, a plastic bag in her hand.

She tossed the bag onto the center console and put her boots back up on the dashboard. Bill fished around the bag. His hand shook as he hung Nightfire around the rearview mirror.

"Are you alright?" Val asked.

"It's fine," he said, firing up the car and throwing it into drive. Val started crying. Bill turned up the stereo.

"I don't-" Val began to say. He saw the muscle twitch as she began to reach for the iPod.

"Stop," Bill said, grabbing her wrist. "Don't speak. Don't do anything. Please."

"Why?" she spat. "Why shouldn't I speak?"

"Because," he said. "Because I have to apologize."

Val gaped. Her arm went limp.

"I haven't been honest," he said. "I don't just drive to be alone. I drive because there's something wrong with me. It hurts to go to sleep, it hurts to wake up. It's nothing to do with you. I just... I wish I'd met you earlier. Before I had this god awful feeling all the time. But it's not your fault. That's it, O.K.?"

The needle surged right. He was so close. If Val could just hang for a few more seconds, he would make it. But her eyes were glistening and her pink lip was shivering and she looked like she was about to explode.

"I feel the same," she said. Bill's eyes flicked up from the needle for a second.

"What?" he said.

"I feel the same," she said. "When I came to New York, I thought I was just feeling homesick. But visiting home didn't help, and the hurt seeped in deeper. And there's only one thing that eases it."

The metallic taste of the shift was already pooling in the base of Bill's mouth like mercury. The engine shook and crackled.

"Val," he muttered. "Please. You're killing me."

"It's being with you," she said. "And you know that. Why else would I come here to find you, when you treat me so horribly?"

The needle passed 80. The old Nevada highway began to dissolve.

"Maybe," Val said, "I could come with you, on one of your strange drives. That way we could both be satisfied."

"Val," he said as she began to disappear. "That's not how this works."

The Firebird wasn't moving. It had not moved in a long time.

Finding the door unlocked, Bill had thrown down his bike and sat down in the driver's seat. He flicked the pine-tree shaped air freshener. Carrie looked on in awe, still straddling her bike. Her scuffed tennis shoes rested on the dirt floor. Her hair was plastered to the side of her face, and the t-shirt she wore under her shortalls stuck to her skin.

They had ridden their way outside the city on country roads and found this old barn off a dirt path. It was charred from fire, roof half-caved in. "What's up with the painting on the hood?" Carrie said, frowning. "It's creepy." Bill shook his head.

"There's no one around," he said. "Come on. Check it out."

He was off script already. That was O.K. That was the plan. Carrie eased herself into the passenger seat.

Bill pulled her close and kissed her, hard.

The kiss is way ahead of schedule. They are supposed to sit there, in the Firebird, talking until the sun goes down. Then he kisses her, after they've rested and cooled off. But he doesn't want to wait. He shouldn't have to. He has sacrificed so much for this drive. So he kisses her, savoring the salt of her sweat, the smell of her sunburned body.

She wrenched away.

"What are you doing?" she said, eyes flashing.

"I don't want to miss any time with you," Bill said. "Please." He leaned to kiss her again and she turned away. He grabbed a handful of her black hair. This was the only summer it was shaggy. Soon she would cut it short, keep it like that forever. But here he could run his fingers through it. He pressed his lips against hers, and for a moment her lips parted.

She bit down. Bill gasped and pulled away. Blood trickled from the corner of her mouth. Carrie's chest heaved.

"You're acting weird," she croaked. "I have to go." She kicked open the passenger door and went back to her bike. "Carrie," he said, dumbstruck as she picked up her bike and shook off the stray bits of dirt and straw.

"Stay away from me," she shouted. He ran his hand through his sweat soaked hair. She swung her leg over her bike.

"Carrie, stop," he said, getting out of the car. "Come back. You don't understand what's happening here."

She kicked off and put her feet to the pedals. He ran after her, out the barn door, into the harsh sunlight. "Stop!" he screamed. "Just stop! You don't understand! This is why I've been night driving all these years! It's all been so I can get back to you, in this moment!"

He grabbed the strap of her shortalls, yanking her back before she could pull away. She fell off the bike, into the dirt, screaming. She slashed at him with nails, kicked at him with dirty tennis shoes.

"You can't do this to me!" he screamed. "You're in my fucking mind!" He grabbed her throat and pinned her down to the ground. Tears streamed down her cheeks, mingling with mud and blood. Her eyes were so beautiful. Her hair was so black.

"You're all I have," he seethed. "How can you do this to me?" She clawed at his wrist. She was gasping for breath, he realized. He loosened his grip and staggered back. His eyes adjusted to the brightness. They were in a fallow field. The sun was low and bright.

"I'm sorry," he gasped. She was coughing, struggling back onto her bike.

His adrenaline surged and he felt the heat of that orange autumn sun wash over him.

"Wait," he said, stepping forward. "Carrie, please, wait-"

He felt the jolt.

He's behind the wheel again, and there's no time to react to what's happening. He clips a minivan at 90 miles per hour, sending it spinning wildly out of control. It rolls across lanes into the path of an eighteen-wheeler. The eighteen-wheeler tries to stop, but it ends up vaporizing the van in a confetti-burst of shredded plastic and metal. The trailer goes sideways. Three lanes of traffic slam on their brakes, and there's a cacophony of crunching and crashing. Bill is looking over his shoulder at the carnage when the steel body of the Firebird cuts through a greyhound bus like a knife through aluminum foil. The gas tank ignites. The heat and light feel just for a moment like the kiss of an autumn sun.

He feels the jolt. He's back in the field. Carrie is struggling back onto her bike, tears streaming. She's desperately peddling away.

"Wait," he said, stepping forward. "Carrie, please-"

He's behind the wheel again, and there's no time to react to what's happening. He clips a minivan, sending it spinning wildly out of control. It rolls across lanes into the path of an eighteen-wheeler. The eighteen-wheeler tries to stop, but it ends up vaporizing the van in a confetti-burst of shredded plastic and metal. The trailer goes sideways. Three lanes of traffic slam on their brakes, and there's a cacophony of crunching and crashing. Bill is looking over his shoulder at the carnage when the steel body of the Firebird cuts through a greyhound bus. The heat and light feel just for a moment like the kiss of an autumn sun.

He's back in the field. The heat of that orange autumn sun washes over him.

In the barn, the Firebird is still and silent. The woman on the hood smiles softly.

A REIGN OF THUNDER
—Part One—

Wayne Kyle Spitzer

It happened *pow,* like that. One minute he'd been blasting through the Arizona desert and listening to Martha and the Vandellas sing "Heat Wave" on the Mustang's AM radio, and the next he was pulling over, rumbling to a stop on the shoulder of State Route 87 and idling in place as the good-looking hitchhiker jogged to catch up with him.

"Man, am I glad to see you," she panted, opening the door—then froze, suddenly, examining the cab, peering into the backseat. "No body parts in that cooler? No murder weapons?"

"Only these," He held up his hands. "Registered as deadly weapons in fifty states. *And* Puerto Rico."

"Is that so?" She laughed, appearing relieved, then climbed in and shut the door. "So where you headed, Deadly Hands?"

"New Mexico. Albuquerque."

"That'll do." She took one of his hands and examined it. "Nah, these are too pretty." She traced his fingers, studying them. "A dentist's, maybe. Or a lab technician." When he didn't say anything, she added: "No? Something creative, then. Nebulous. An artist, maybe. Or a photographer."

He shifted in his seat uncomfortably, unsure whether he was getting creeped out by her touch and directness—or a hard-on. He glanced her up and down quickly: the slender figure, the long, dark hair—the brown eyes like a doe in heat. Definitely a hard-on. "Look, I—"

"*A writer,* I think," she said, suddenly, and let go of his hand. "Ha! Am I warm?"

He opened his mouth to speak but closed it immediately, seeing only Heller and the office at 123 Wilshire Blvd—the cheap suit, the shit-eating grin—his hard-on withering like a prune in September.

"No," he said at last, gripping the gearshift, pushing in the clutch. "You're cold. Cold as fucking Pluto."

And then they were moving, crossing the rumble strip and picking up speed, the engine growling, leaping up, the sweltering sun beating down, as she looked at him, curiously, quizzically, and he tried to ignore her. As the mercury in the little thermometer on the dash topped 90 degrees—and kept climbing.

"So what's your story?" she asked, shouting over the wind and the radio, which was too loud, too tinny. He turned it down.

"My story?" He laughed. "I'm not the one who was hitchhiking through the Sonoran Desert."

She smiled self-deprecatingly. "Yeah, there is that." She hung her head back so that her dark hair billowed out the window. "I was at an artist's colony—the Desert Muse." She smiled again, bitterly, it seemed. "Or the Desert Ruse, as I call it. Ever heard of it?"

He shook his head.

"Yeah, well, it's where a bunch of grad students hang out with their professors for a week and study the fine arts. You know, like how to out-snark the other pimply kids ... or fuck your professor."

He glanced at her sidelong, raising an eyebrow.

"Okay, so maybe not fuck him. But definitely give him something to think about. You know, like when he's handing out teaching internships."

He nodded slowly, exaggeratedly. "Ah."

"Ah. So I just bugged out. I didn't want to play anymore. And now I'm heading home. Back to Miami."

He drove, listening, the wind buffeting his hair, which was graying at the temples. She couldn't have been more than, say, what? Twenty-five? Twenty-six? "Yeah? And?"

"And that's all you get. At least until I know something about you. Your name, for instance."

He accelerated, he wasn't sure why, focusing on the road. "Cooper," he said, finally. "Cooper Black. But, please, call me 'Coup'—everyone does."

"Cooper—Coup. *Black?* Cooper Black? Like the font?"

"Just like the font."

"Well, that's different." She fell silent for a moment, watching the scenery pass. "I'm Tess, by the way. Tess Baker." She added, "Please. Go on."

Cooper only exhaled. "No, no, no, *that's it.* I was just coming back from L.A. when I saw you with your thumb out." He turned the radio back up but got only static. "That's really all there is to it. Just a guy on a road trip."

Neither said anything as the radials droned and the radio hissed.

"I think you went there for a reason ... and it didn't go so well. That's what I think." She waited as he fiddled with the dial. "Can't find your channel there, Coup?"

"No, Doctor Laura, I can't, actually. Can't seem to find much of anything. And I went there, if you must know, because I'd sold a book to Roman House and the editor I was working with had a heart attack—he just keeled, okay? So I had to meet this new asshole, who couldn't stand me *or* the book, and who cancelled the entire project. And then ..."

He looked at her and found her arching an eyebrow quizzically.

"Then I hit him. All right? Right in the old kisser. And then I turned his desk over and threw his banker's light, you know, the kind with the faux gold plating and green glass shade—"

She nodded impatiently.

"—right through the window. And then I ran like a rabbit, straight to my car and out of L.A., after which I passed this really good-looking hitchhiker who peppered me with questions until I started going bugfuck. Okay? All right? You happy?"

"I like a man who can open up," she said.

"I'm not opening up. I'm trying to—"

And then they heard it, the whir of a siren, after which he looked through his rear-view mirror and she out the back window to see a brown and white State Patrol vehicle following them dangerously close, its windshield reflecting the sun like knives and its red and blue lights flashing, telling them to pull over.

"It's just not my fucking day," he marveled, still looking in the mirror, even as Tess placed a hand on his leg—close to his crotch, he noticed—and said: "But it could be, Coup. It still could be." —before her eyes expanded like saucers and she shrieked, shouting, "Look out!"

And he looked ahead in time to see a brown blur, a large mouse, he thought, or a kitten, which had been scurrying across the road, vanish beneath the filthy hood.

It all happened so quickly that it wasn't even clear, at least at first, *what* had happened, other than he'd slammed on the brakes to avoid hitting the creature and caused the police car to ram them from behind—like a wrecking ball, it seemed, knocking them forward.

And then there they were, stalled at the side of the road in front of a partially accordioned police car (while parked over an almost certainly dead cat, possibly a rodent) and feeling their necks; even as Coup glanced in the rear-view mirror and saw the officer storming toward them—his service weapon drawn.

"Oh, not good," said Tess, shrinking down in her seat, as Cooper held up his hands and offered assurances. "It's okay—everything's going to be fine. There's nothing to—"

"Get out of the car and get on the ground! Now!"

"Jesus," said Coup.

"Yeah. Shouldn't he at least be asking us if we're all right?"

"Do it!"

They did it, easing open their doors and hurrying to get on the ground, putting their hands behind their backs, making of themselves nice little arrestable bundles.

"Look, Officer, I can explain every ..."

"Shut up! Shut up and stay on the ground! Don't move!"

They didn't move—but stayed precisely as they were, their hearts pounding, their blood racing, as the cop keyed his mic:

"530 to Dispatch, request back-up at State Route 87 and 19, collision with civilian vehicle, possible DUI. Over."

"Possible DUI?" Coup craned his neck to look at him. "Where in the hell did you get—"

"Shut up and stay on the ground! Keep your hands behind your back!" And into his mic: "530 to Dispatch, did you copy? Over."

But there was nothing, no reply whatsoever, just static—like the Mustang's AM radio. Coup craned his neck again, this time in the opposite direction: And no vehicles, either. Come to think of it, there'd been nothing since he'd picked up the girl, not even so much as a semi, always so ubiquitous.

He strained to peer skyward, the sun stabbing at his eyes. And no air traffic. No contrails to fuel the conspiracy theorists—nothing. Just a pale, blue dome, without even a cloud.

He froze as gravel crunched beneath the cop's shoes, half expecting a boot on his neck, but quickly realized the man was moving away from him, not toward him, back toward his car.

"I'm scared, Coup," said Tess, her voice sounding small, distant. "I'm really scared."

"I know," he said, the sweat pouring down his forehead, stinging his eyes. "I am too. But it'll be all right. Just, you know, chill, as they say. He's called for back-up. That's a good thing."

"Witnesses," she said. "Maybe a commanding officer."

"Exactly. Just hang tight. I know it's hot."

"I'll be okay." She added: "Thanks, Coup."

He grunted. "What do you mean?"

"I don't know. Just—thanks. For being here. For looking out for me. Like a big brother, almost. Or a fa—"

"*Shht,* he's coming," he said—suddenly, urgently.

The world just sat, silently.

"But I don't hear any—"

"Sorry, false alarm. Must have been my own foot, or something."

And then they waited.

How much time passed would have been difficult to say: maybe it was only a few minutes—say, ten or fifteen—and maybe it was a half hour; regardless, when they at last climbed to their feet and walked to the officer's car, they found him nowhere in sight. He had, quite simply, just vanished without a trace.

"But ... that's impossible," said Tess, shielding her eyes, scanning the horizon,. "He couldn't possibly have walked that far—could he?"

Coup appeared troubled as he stood next to her and did likewise. "It's possible ... but it sure as hell ain't likely." He looked at the patrol car, the door of which still hung open, and his eyes seized upon the shotgun—which glinted between the seats like black gold. "Maybe someone picked him up. But why would he leave in the first place? And why would he leave *that* just sitting there for anyone to take?"

He looked to where the keys hung from the ignition. "Not to mention the car itself?"

"There's no footprints," said Tess, examining the ground. She looked up at him as though she felt suddenly ill. "Nothing leading away. Just ours and his walking to and from ..." She paused, her lower lip trembling. "How is that possible, Coup? And not just him but—where is everybody else? Where are the other cars? How in ..."

And then she just *broke* suddenly and rushed into his arms, and they remained like that for several minutes, during which time he scanned the sky, and, to his deep relief, spied a passenger jet arching glimmeringly across the sky, its contrail just as white and reassuring as angel dust.

"Look, there, see," He released her abruptly and spun her around. "We're not in the Twilight Zone, after all. Hey, yo, Freedom Bird! We're down here!" He waved his arms back and forth. "Give us a lift! Albuquerque or bust!"

Yet there was something odd about the plane's trajectory he hadn't initially noticed—or had he? For it truly was *arching*, which is to say it wasn't crossing the sky so much as it was ... falling from it. Yes, yes, he could see now that was true, as he disengaged from Tess and paced through the scrub, tracking the jet as it curved gracefully in the sun— to finally plummet straight into the far hills, where it vanished like a specter in a plume of fiery smoke.

And then he was gripping the shotgun and trying to wrest it from its rack; but, finding it locked, had to search the car for a key: upon which, realizing there were none that would fit, he located a small button just beneath the seat and depressed it— freeing the weapon.

"I don't think that's a good idea," said Tess as she tailed him back to the Mustang, but he ignored her until they were again seated inside, after which he turned to her and said, briskly, "Maybe it is and maybe it isn't, but I'm doing it, okay?"

And it was on the tip of her lips to respond when they heard the sound: a kind of muffled whimper—something between a chirp and a meow—coming from outside. Coming from beneath the car.

"Oh my God, Coup. The cat ..."

"It was a *rat,* I think."

"Whatever it is; it's ... still alive. Listen."

And he did listen—and quickly determined that, whatever it was, it was either in great pain or scared out of its wits.

And then they were both scrambling, out of the car and into the heat and glare, and what they saw next was something neither of them would forget—for it was both portent and prelude to everything which lie ahead.

It was two things above all else: adorable and almost dead. It was also attached to the top of the tire like a vise (where it had taken refuge after the near collision), its little claws dug into the rubber like a cat's and its dark eyes regarding them fearfully—and yet somehow bravely. Still, it was not a cat (or a kitten) in spite of its claws, nor was it a mouse, however over-sized. What it was, quite simply, was something unknown; although what Coup thought it resembled most was a mongoose, albeit clearly still in its infant stage. Nor did it seem to be dangerous, as Tess found out when she touched it against Coup's advice and it merely licked her fingers—or tried to—its sandpapery tongue just as dry as the dead.

"It's this heat," she said, finally, stroking its neck and back. "It's seriously dehydrated." She looked at Coup. "Whatever it is, I don't think it has very long."

"It needs water," he said. "And it needs it fast."

He stood and looked into the backseat; at the cooler he'd picked up from Walmart before heading out to L.A. "And we gotta bring his temperature down. Can you move him, you think?"

"I think so, yes. If he'll let go of the tire."

Coup took a spare shirt from the back and shook it out, then opened the cooler and laid it inside. "Most the ice is still good; we'll lay him in here." He picked a Styrofoam cup off the floor. "And see if we can't get him to drink something."

And then, having managed a few sips and been laid in the chest—it had taken both of them to disengage it from the tire—the thing seemed to sleep; as they pulled away from the shoulder and back onto the road (although where they should go was another question entirely) and decided to name it "Rikki-Tik"—after Kipling's famous mongoose.

They hadn't traveled far, however, when they encountered more evidence that something wasn't right—with the road, with the traffic (or lack thereof), with *the world.*

"What's that?" asked Tess as something glinted about a mile ahead, something blue and crumpled, torn, smashed.

"What's what?" he said, and then noticed it: a blue and chrome thing turned over on it side in the middle of the road, a ruined and battered thing. A car.

"Jesus," he said, letting off the gas.

"Mary and Joseph," added Tess. "Christ. Do you think anyone could have ..." She paused, squinting. "Coup, tell me that isn't what I think it is."

But he was seeing it too, and knew that what was splashed down the car's door was *exactly* what she thought it was.

"It's blood, all right." He geared down and brought them slowly alongside the hulk, where he put it in park and inhaled, deeply. He did not, however, shut off the engine.

"Please, God, be empty," said Tess. "I'm not ready for this shit."

Coup sighed. "Why don't you ... check on our friend or something. I'll have a look ."

"Okay."

But he'd barely begun to open his door when a wrinkled hand appeared suddenly, waveringly, amidst the wreckage—and gripped its glass-covered dash. After which Coup reiterated calmly, gently: "Tess, check on our friend." —and climbed out.

To Coup's astonishment, the man—who couldn't have been less than ninety years old—had suffered only minor cuts and abrasions; although his wife, he said, had been killed (which was weird, to say the least, since he was the only one in the car). Beyond that, though, he hadn't had much to say—nor did Coup blame him—as they rumbled from the scene and continued east; indeed, he seemed to still be in state of shock. One thing, however, was woefully clear, and that was that at his age (and level of dementia) he shouldn't have been driving in the first place.

"Maybe she was thrown clear," said Tess as she buckled him in next to the ice chest, her tight Levi shorts merely inches from Coup's head. "It was obviously a horrific accident; although it is strange that there was no other car. Could they have had a blowout, you think?"

"The short answer is 'no,'" said Coup matter-of-factly. "That car's tires were good. As for being thrown clear—no way. I searched the entire area. There was nothing. Not unless the coyotes carried her away."

"Well, there you—"

"The coyotes didn't carry her away, Tess."

"Look, I don't know," she protested as she helped the man dig out his wallet—it was fat and had been causing him discomfort, was her guess.

All of which went out the window when he removed a picture from it and handed it to her: a picture of himself and his wife when they were much, much younger—or so she'd presumed, at least until she saw the timestamp in the lower right corner of the frame. A timestamp which read: October 15, 2017.

"*This is nuts,*" said Coup, looking at it, before handing it back. "All of this is just stark-raving ..."

But he never finished the sentence, for they were approaching another vehicle, three other vehicles, to be precise, all of which were ditched at the side of the road as though their drivers had simply fallen asleep.

"They're empty, every single one," whispered Tess as they passed the vehicles at a virtual crawl. "Just like the cop car. Just like this guy's wife. It's almost as if—"

"Don't say it," said Coup.

"Well, it's true, isn't it?"

"We don't know that yet—"

"It's like they just disappeared! Just *poof!* Gone!"

"Tess—"

"Goddamn it, Coup! Lying to ourselves about it isn't going to—"

"Some of them did," said the old man suddenly, rendering them speechless, even as Tess turned around and Coup looked into the rear-view mirror. "Vanished just like ghosts, like they'd never existed at all. I know because I saw it with my own eyes. But that's not what happened to my wife."

They just looked at him, nobody saying anything. It was, in a sense, as if he'd been reborn—still as old as Methuselah but suddenly alert and aware; enough so that he'd become acutely aware of his condition and surroundings and seemed to be entranced by the sight of his own liver-spotted hand, which he studied as though it wasn't his at all but a total stranger's.

At last he said, "No. No. Because you see, some disappeared. And some, well, I guess some have or will end up like me. But my wife ..." He paused, looking first at Coup and then at Tess, his eyes ancient, haunted, possessed almost. "My wife was *eaten.*"

After which they faced forward again and didn't say anything for a long time, not until they passed the green and white sign indicating food and gas via the next exit, at which they looked at each other and nodded at almost the same instant, then touched hands as if to brace themselves for what they might find there.

102

It was called the Border Rendezvous and as best Coup could figure it, it was a Union 76 gas station on crack. What else was there to make of a place with a giant Mexican bandit named "Benito the Bandido" standing over its drive—his legs bowed absurdly and his hands gripping the titular sign— or boasting in its other signage of being home to the world famous Dingo Dog ("Have a Dingo, Gringo!") and the "largest indoor reptile exhibit in the U.S.?"

"Jesus," said Tess as they drove between the statue's gargantuan legs, "Where were the P.C. Police when they built this?"

"Just a gleam in someone's eye," said Coup, maneuvering the Mustang around a lengthy pump island (which was more befitting an actual truck stop than a glorified gas station/food mart). "Probably one of those professors at the Desert Ruse." He added: "Don't knock it. They'll be cold water and air-conditioning. Not to mention a big TV."

She looked at him, struck by his mentioning of the Desert Ruse. He *listened.* She wasn't used to that. "Yeah, but ..." She looked at the building's front windows doubtfully. "Will there be a signal?"

"That," he said, as they rumbled up to those windows and stopped, "is the 64-thousand dollar question." He shut off the engine and exhaled. "Okay. I'll take our furry friend if you can assist Mr.—?"

"Becker," said the old man. "Henry Becker. And I don't need a nurse to get out of a car, thank you. I was thirty-four just an hour ago."

Tess looked at Cooper but he just shrugged. One didn't know whether to laugh or to cry.

They all got out, Coup fetching the ice chest while Tess walked behind Becker, her arms at the ready, and they went into the store, where they were greeted immediately by a cacophony of voices—and saw a large group gathered in front of the counter.

"Any one of you a doctor?" someone snapped, having turned at the sound of door chimes—a large black man with a shiny head and long gray beard (a trucker, maybe, or a biker, although Coup hadn't noticed any bikes out front). "Or do you have any medicine? Prescription meds, opioids, muscle relaxers ..."

The three of them just froze.

"Speak up!"

"No, nothing," said Coup—he couldn't help but notice that Tess had gripped his arm instinctively— and added, "What is it? What's going on?"

There was a sound like liquid splattering the floor and a woman in a red dress turned around, cupping her mouth. "Oh my God. Can't someone just kill it?"

"Now, wait a minute—"

"She's right, you know. Who has a gun?" said the big man—adding, when no one responded, "Come on! This has got to end!"

An animal, thought Coup. *Someone's animal is dying—probably from this heat. Jesus.*

It was on the tip of his lips to say he did, in the car, when someone beat him to it; a wiry little man in a cowboy hat and wife-beater (who had also turned at the chimes), who said, plaintively, "I have one."

"Jesus, Coup, look," said Tess, nodding toward the ceiling, toward the massive flat screen mounted above and behind the counter, and he nearly leapt with joy when he saw that it was not in fact broadcasting static but actual imagery—or at least the CNN logo, which filled the screen—and that someone was talking: Anderson Cooper, perhaps, although it was difficult to say over the commotion at the counter. Coup caught only "extreme weather ranging from sudden heat waves to flash ice-storms all across the country" before hearing another splattering of liquid and the people at the counter gasp, after which a single shot rang out and he jumped.

And then it was over—whatever it was—and the animal, whatever it had been, was dead, surely, and Tess ran to him and collided with his shoulder even as the room returned to some kind of normalcy and the voice on the TV continued: "... the fact is we just don't know. *I* don't know. I don't know where my family is or if they're safe. I don't know if we have a President—or if he's simply vanished. I don't know where our first responders are, or our law enforcement, to say nothing of the military, or why so many of our friends and loved ones have disappeared. All I know is—"

And then static broke across the screen like a gunshot—pow, like *that*—and their connection to the rest of the world was lost; and the room fell silent, or nearly so, for a woman sitting at one of the booths was sobbing and the static continued to hiss.

That's when Coup first noticed it, the blood which was so dark as to be almost black, spreading from the small gap beneath the counter, pooling around people's shoes—and set down the ice chest, embracing Tess briefly before moving toward the gathering and peering over the fixture himself.

Where he saw something so strange and terrible, so grotesque, that his mind could not at first accept it: a thing not only without analog to the natural world (at least insofar as he understood it) but which seemed a purposeful mockery. A thing, in short, which was neither man nor animal, and yet, somehow, a tangle of both.

A thing from which he shielded a little girl as she inexplicably tried to join him and whose dead, randomly placed eyes—two of them small, blue, human, two others as large and slit-pupiled as any serpent's—gazed emptily into space.

Had Coup anticipated how unbearable the silence would become he wouldn't have sought out the remote and silenced the TV, nor encouraged Tess to take Rikki-Tik to the restroom and clean him up.

And yet, Christ, what was there to say? They were strangers, all of them—even he and Tess were strangers—who among them even knew the other's name, much less anything about what was going on or what the thing lying behind the counter was? When at last he spoke he did so quietly, almost reverentially, offering only his name and where he'd been heading, hoping the others gathered around the counter would follow suit— which, after a moment, they did, slowly, hesitantly.

"Rory Holmes," said the big man, "long-haul trucker, enroute to Los Angeles from Laredo, when—when all this happened."

"Elliott Giles," said the wiry guy in the wife-beater, "disabled veteran. Not any war, just—just the service. Enroute to Phoenix from Las Cruces." He paused, his lower lip trembling. "I—I only did what had to be done."

"You're good. You're all good, man," said Rory, clapping him on the back, startling him. "You done right."

The introductions continued:

"Long Nguyen. Civil engineer. Atlanta to San Diego."

"Ashley May. Phoenix from Cedar City. Utah."

"Cameron Reeves. Ah—" The twenty-something year-old hesitated. "Immigration activist enroute to the new wall at El Paso." He paused, appearing self-conscious. "From Washington. That's my group." He indicated a trio of young people near the booths.

"D.C.?" asked Rory.

"State," said Cameron. "Seattle."

"Ah. The Great White North."

"Sure. I guess."

"Carson Bates," blurted a heavyset man abruptly, squaring his beefy shoulders. "Carrot-topped farmer cum crop-duster; and all around daredevil." He glanced at Cameron and tweaked his MAGA hat. "And a proud supporter of President Donald J. Tucker."

"You don't say," said Coup. The hat alone was pretty hard to ignore.

Cameron just shrugged.

That left only two in the immediate group who hadn't spoken; the attractive woman in the red dress (who seemed to have recovered) and a young man of Native American heritage who introduced himself only as "Johnny—from Tucson."

"Kate Patel," said the woman at length, "CEO, Desert Smoke Vapors. Enroute to L.A. from Austin." Her voice lowered slightly. "And about to get underway again."

"It's your apocalypse," said Coup. "And a warm welcome to all."

And yet the silence reasserted itself as they watched the tangle of flesh cool and bleed; its eight limbs stiffening like driftwood and its eyes staring in four different directions, its chaos of muscle and bone settling, until, spying a nametag amidst the riot of fabric and tissue, Coup said, "It's the clerk. He or she—has been *combined* with something. Like a lizard. Or a crocodile. Look,"

He pointed to where a partial human face had emerged from the mangle, its mouth stretched in a hideous grimace, its right cheek morphed like clay, its gray flesh blending seamlessly back into the beast—the monitor lizard. The crocodile, whatever.

"Right there, at the animal's neck. See it?"

"Like they were baked together in a fucking microwave," said Rory.

"Or melted—like nachos." said Elliott.

"More like fused," said Long. "Blended to form a single entity ... a single amalgamate."

"Like Brundlefly," whispered Ashley.

Coup hadn't quite caught that.

She blushed a little self-consciously. "Like *The Fly.* You know, that movie from the '80s, with Jeff Goldblum."

Everyone just looked at her.

"The remake—of the original black and white. Jesus. *The Fly.*"

"I *know* the movie," said Coup. "But what's—"

"When the guy who built the transportation pod gets drunk and tests it on himself, and the fly gets caught in the matrix ..."

"... and they get fused together." He looked down at the thing, at the four human limbs and the four reptilian ones, at the four dead eyes all pointed in different directions. "Jesus ... But what could—"

"That's not all," said Long.

He went around the counter and approached the corpse—his shoes squelching in the blood and gruel—then hitched up his pants and knelt. "This foot here, for example—"

"Don't touch it!" said Ashley.

He paused, fingertips hovering.

"She's right, you know," said Rory. "Who knows what that thing might be carrying."

He traced the scales, his finger suspended just above them. "See this? Kind of like a big bird's talon, isn't it? Not much like a lizard—more like an ostrich, or an emu. But what's really curious is this, right here." He indicated a single scythe-like claw, about three inches in length, and curved like a scimitar. "Because it's retractable, see?" He laughed slightly. "Like your cat's. And it's sickled-shaped. Which means—"

"Look, ah, Bill Nye," interrupted Carson, shouldering past Coup, displacing him with his bulk. "Is there a point to any of this? Or are you just showing off your American education?"

Coup raised an eyebrow.

"Well, yes, there is," said Long. He appeared vaguely stupefied. "The point is: no animal like this currently exists."

Carson just looked at him—like a big, dopey John Candy—appearing amused. "It's not? Well, what is it, then?" He looked at the others as if for support. "Is it Mothra?" He laughed.

"Whatever it is, we can't just leave it here," said Elliott.

Coup looked outside, at the landscaped berm on the south end of the lot. "We'll bury it there, by the water—"

"Look, you guys can do whatever you want," Kate interrupted, "but I'm not touching that thing." Her keys rattled as she removed them from her purse. "Besides, I've got a board meeting to attend." She moved toward the doors. "Apocalypse or no apocalypse."

"Now wait a—" Rory began.

"Are you—" said Elliott.

"Is that really a good idea?" asked Coup, which at last caused her to turn around.

"I don't know, is it?" she said, and slung the purse over her shoulder. "Why don't you ask *him*?" She indicated Long. "He seems to know everything."

"He's right," said Rory. "It's not a good idea."

"It's the only idea," she snapped determinedly. She patted her purse warningly. "And don't even *think* about ..."

But they were no longer looking at her— gazing instead at something which had swooped into view outside, something which seemed for an instant almost to hover—its muscles and ligaments twitching, making a thousand adjustments, its stretched membranes undulating, its talons outstretched—before it smashed against the glass like some great, dark kite (cracking it three different ways) and hit the ground violently, scrambling and flapping, leaping and taking wing again, disappearing from sight. All of which happened so fast that the woman in the red dress, having leapt away suddenly, didn't appear to have even seen it, much less identified it, and only said, finally, "What was that?" And then laughed. "Are we under attack by wild turkeys, for fuck's sake?"

And then the incident was over and the only sounds were those of the commercial refrigerators humming and the fountain drink regulators hissing, and no one said anything, even when Tess burst back into the room and said, breathlessly, "Jesus, what's going on?"

"In Bumfuck, Arizona?" said Kate acidly. "Nothing. Kate is leaving, that's what's going on. Ta-ta. Let me know when it's time for the reunion."

And yet this time she was answered, and by an unexpected voice, a voice as strong and confident as any thirty-four-year-old.

A voice which belonged to the old-young man himself, Henry Becker.

"You want to leave, young lady? Go right ahead," he said, approaching her, each step small, cautious, carefully considered. "But know this. Denial has its limits. And in this case, that limit is exactly where those doors stand." He closed to within a few feet of her before she touched her purse and said, "That's close enough." —causing him to take a step back. He continued: "It might be closer than that, considering these ... things ... can appear out of nowhere." He turned and indicated the amalgamate. "That poor bastard, for example. His only crime was being in the wrong place at the wrong time. Because there's something you need to understand, Miss—"

"Patel,"

"Miss Patel. And that is that for every person gone to this—this phenomena—and you must have seen the empty cars ... something else has, shall we say, *arrived.*"

She seemed to hesitate, her eyes blinking, her attitude faltering.

"And one of these things, Miss Patel, is outside now. Probably on the roof. We—we saw it, you understand, while you were turned around. But it was aiming for you. And it is only because of those thin doors that you are still here."

She looked at him passively, almost intimately—as though he'd reached her; as though she were about to change her mind. And then the moment was gone and she was shoving through the doors, letting in the sweltering heat, reminding everyone of what lie just beyond the glass, striding for her car while her red dress flowed freely behind.

"Jesus, we can't just—" Coup started to say, and lurched forward—but was restrained by Tess, even as Kate made it to her car and opened the door, tossing in her purse, then turned toward the store and shrugged nonchalantly—before gripping her elbow and flipping everyone off.

"See? Big girl panties," said Tess, and Coup could have just kissed her—when there was a huge, black blur at the corner of his eye and someone gasped; and he turned to see that Kate was gone—just *gone*. He blinked and she was there again, dangling from the flying thing's talons, folding as it lighted upon the orange Union '76 ball; offering up her intestines as it thrust its long, thin beak into her long, thin body.

And then Tess was screaming and he was trying to calm her—as yet another great kite swooped in and lighted upon a streetlight; and still another after that, lighting upon a utility pole; and still one more, which glided in like a jet until its talons touched down in the middle of the lot and it ran on them briefly before dropping to all fours and crawling the rest of the way to the windows.

"Jesus, they're everywhere," said Rory, moving to within several feet of the glass. He looked at the creature on the ground as it stared in at them. "Like seagulls after breadcrumbs."

"And we're the breadcrumbs," said Tess.

She watched as yet more arrived and a commotion broke out atop the '76 sign, where a larger bird attacked the smaller one and wrested its prey away (part of it, anyway) before beating its wings and soaring off—strewing body parts, causing those on the ground to scramble and to squabble amongst themselves.

"It's an outright feeding frenzy," said Elliott, stepping up next to Coup. He looked at the creature on the other side of the window even as it was joined by a multitude of others. "Jesus. Look at their eyes."

But Coup had already noticed—that strange glow that wasn't really a glow; that backlit fogginess, as though they were blind or perhaps even rabid.

"Like zombies," said Rory. "Like flying fucking voodoo zombies." He twisted his body, staring at the sky. "And what the hell is that?"

Coup followed his gaze to where a borealis shimmered like iridescent curtains: its colors shifting and blending, creating hues he'd never before seen (and which hurt his mind), its scale unimaginable. "It's like the whole world's gone crazy."

"Worse," said Henry, and steadied himself against a fixture, "we're trapped. If not before than certainly now." He looked outside to where more and more birds were arriving, crowding the lot like flies, making a sea of gray. "They know there's food here."

Coup watched as a ripple moved through that sea—as though the birds had heard something. As though something had spooked them. "What's that?" he said.

And then everything just exploded—as the birds scattered and took flight and what seemed like stones rattled the glass and foodstuffs began bursting and it became apparent that what they were hearing was gunfire. As everyone hit the floor and the room was pocked by bullets, and Coup blanketed Tess' body with his own.

As he looked over his shoulder and saw the M1 Abrams tank jouncing into the lot, its machine gun flashing and its exhaust ports belching black smoke—its great, flat turret rotating, pointing directly at them.

A Reign of Thunder
will continue next issue

TECHNOLUTION

Eleanor Mourante

A sea of soulless eyes filled the screen, hands clutching signs and red flags with the Lion Guard emblem. The broadcaster talked about enthusiasm for the forthcoming free elections and ensuring our nation's place on the world stage.

I turned the program off and cleaned the kitchen. Nothing I needed to see; I'd been counting the days until our first election day in a decade. January 6th, acknowledging the day Loyalists overthrew the usurper.

This time, January 6th would be the day when those of us who'd hid in the shadows got a chance to take our nation back.

The display in my left eye flickered. It lost primary colors, turning into a grayscale image of my kitchen with black dots splattered over it. My EyeScreen blanked out and I stumbled into the countertop.

The sharp quartz edge jabbed just below my ribcage. Bile rose in my throat and filled my mouth with a putrid acidity, making me want to gag.

I saw white. It felt like someone stabbed me with an icepick through the skull, above my left ear. The bone quivered from the pressure as the pick's tip dug its way toward the temporal lobe.

The display in my right eye—which was working—pinged, telling me I was a slightly cool 96.7°F. Nausea coursed through my body and I pushed bile down my throat. I'd just cleaned the cornflower blue cabinets, white-with-gray-swirl counters, and gray tile floors, and I wasn't about to let a technical malfunction undo my efforts.

My display turned a sharp yellow. The brightness assaulted my skull. White-hot embers shot through my head, the pick morphing into a corkscrew, twisting, turning in small circles that sent shockwaves throughout my brain and down my spine.

My nails dug into the underside of the quartz, my knees buckled, and I slumped toward the floor.

A straight line of pain cut across my head, as though a guillotine had sliced into it, but the blade stuck three quarters of the way through, unable to sever the top completely. A sheet of cold steel shivered against the brain tissue it had sliced apart.

I recalled severe headaches before the EyeScreen implantation, the promise of technologically advanced healthcare. Need glasses? Not anymore. Chemical imbalance in the brain? Automatically regulated.

What I felt was an echo of my memories of migraines.

Times twenty.

Lania breezed into the room. She seemed to float, as though the wind making the sheer olive drapes flutter had lifted and carried her through the open patio doors. Everything Lania did seemed effortless.

My breath caught in my throat, the way it always did when my daughter appeared.

Lania's voice sparkled when she laughed. Some might call it a trick of the EyeScreen, a sentimental touch from one of the upgrades, but I knew that wasn't true. I'd heard and seen light every time Lania laughed or cried or cooed or spoke since she was a child.

Long before I'd complied with mandatory EyeScreen installation.

My light in the darkness. My motivation for resisting the mindlessness sweeping the nation. My hope for the future.

Lania saw me, hanging over the edge of the counter. "Did you turn your alerts off again?" Her voice was soft and light, like late afternoon sun on a spring day.

How did she always sound like she didn't have a care in the world?

She pressed the side of my head and the pain stopped. The right screen went blank before the regular display returned. I stood up straight. My knees shook a little, but I commanded the tap to run, cupped some water with my hand, and splashed it over my mouth and chin.

"Mia, wet wipe," Lania said. The Manufactured Intelligence Asset—MIA—dispensed a wipe.

She'd insisted on making the wall unit's acronym a proper name. I'd let her, basking in the joy she expressed over modernizing, telling myself giving it a name meant she was holding on to her humanity.

Before that, Lania's friends described my home as retro, while Lania laughed and said it was absolutely antique and not fit for the nationalist era.

She gave me the wipe and I cleaned my face.

"Dispose," I told the sink. Water swirled in from the jets under its rim, the refuse trap opened, and I tossed the wipe in. It rushed down the drain.

Lania clasped my hand, her skin softer than cotton balls and smoother than silk. "I keep trying to tell you."

"I just wanted to clean—"

"Oh, silly! That's what Mia and Asa are for."

Asa. Administration and Sanitation Android. The machine that was supposed to manage the house and keep everything in order.

Limited only by humans that refused to use it. Like me.

"I like cleaning. It's good to stay busy."

"Plant flowers, walk, visit friends. Enjoy yourself and let the machines do the work."

I couldn't disagree with Lania, not when she looked at me with her soft smile and mirth-filled eyes. How an antiquated grump like me had been blessed with such a beautiful progressive positive thinker remained a mystery.

Lania slipped her arm through mine and led me outside. Her friends lounged on the patio, the late December day unseasonably warm. "Updates regulate the software. You can also limit your tech time. They have that feature because of addiction."

Lania settled on a recliner. An ancient stone wall embraced the patio, a wall I'd refused to let the Advancement Council tear down.

I argued it shielded my virtuous daughter from the prying eyes of the boy next door; the council applauded my values and let the wall remain.

It was my only post-Technolution victory. The Sanders boy had never given Lania a second glance; I felt guilty for using him, but no harm came from the wall petition and I'd gotten my way.

"I remember that from smartphones. Some people had screen addiction."

"How positively quaint," Vanna said, tossing her long, brown hair back from her face.

"How awkward." Melanka raked her fingers through her raven mane. "Imagine needing to carry a box everywhere."

"They weren't even see-through," Lania said. "You could only see the display! It would positively disrupt your life. Thank goodness for Technolution."

I should have named her Joy. I'd chosen another name, but it wasn't an option. I went from nine months pregnant and casting my ballot to the uprising and heard the new rules after giving birth. I couldn't bear to take the name of our newly-declared Founding Mother, and settled for the abbreviation instead.

Not exactly rebellion, but my own small way of avoiding compliance in the wake of the chaos.

I'd been absolved of so much as a young, first-time mother in the hospital, newly widowed, white, fertile, bearing a child on what our leader called our Reclamation Day.

Factors that covered a multitude of sins in the new Republic.

"If you get AudioBots implanted, the EyeScreen stabilizes," Lania said.

"Fixing one piece of tech with another?" I frowned.

Vanna sat up. "Maybe the systems don't work as well with people your age. Did you have the removables?"

It was my turn to laugh. "We called those glasses. People had them perched on their face so they could look through the lenses."

"However did that work?" Melanka asked.

"There were two big circles in front of your eyes, connected by a plastic or metal piece that rested on your nose. And then arms from the circles went back and hooked on your ears."

"Ghastly." Melanka shuddered. "I can't believe anyone ever had to wear such primitive technology."

"Oh, glasses weren't electronic."

"They were before the first surgery was mandatory, right, Mom?" Lania said.

"That's right. LensScreens. People left smartphones behind. It was more convenient to wear glasses with a computer in them."

"I, for one, am relieved I was born in a civilized era. I never had to experience Partisan Combat." Melanka shuddered. "Why, Ms. Carter, you probably knew socialists!"

I tapped my temple, blinking away the tears that pricked at the corners of my eyes. "The hearing thing helps this work better?"

"Yes," Lania said. "I'll take you to see about the AudioBots. Not tonight, though."

"Because you have a date, don't you?" Vanna said. The girls giggled and I escaped to my bedroom.

A date? Who was Lania seeing?

The only date on my mind for weeks had been election day.

Lania took me shopping just after New Year's. Implanting the AudioBots didn't take long, and we included a detour to the shoe shop.

.I went to the fitting area, sat down, and removed my simple, soft, electronic-free trainers. They'd lasted years and were like old friends, and my feet felt naked without them.

Lanie picked them up by the laces and deposited them on a rubbish tray near the mechanical disposal unit. Its moss-colored exterior blended in green shades checkered across the wall, but even without a steel façade I knew what it was. Our world was less flesh, blood, wood, and earth and more machine every day.

It was hard to maintain order with organics, but people could control technology.

Jamie arrived, swept his coiffed hair back with his hand, sat across from me, crossed his legs, leaned over, and touched my knee with his fingertips. "Choosing shoes can be overwhelming."

Lania looked at his hand and a cloud shadowed her normally bright face. "That's why we have constructive limiting," she said.

Her tone was uncharacteristically flat and dark, as though she sensed what I'd long known about my shoe salesman and gladly overlooked. Or did her words seem bleak because she'd used the current government buzzwords?

Jamie squeezed her hand and winked. "Some women appreciate their choices more than others. Why, with your physique, I'm sure you enjoy trying all the latest trends." He let go of her and reached for a box. "Ms. Carter, I do believe I sold you those old trainers, didn't I?"

I nodded. The shadow on Lania's face faded, but she remained silent and watched Jamie.

"These new InsoLutions might seem fussy, but you're going to love them." He set the pair in front of my feet and pointed. "Just put your feet on the insoles."

They looked like a deformed leather octopus. The welt, tongue, toe cap, and other parts splayed out from that padded, foot-shaped insole.

"I just—"

"May I?" Jamie asked.

I nodded. He placed each foot on the shoes.

The unfolded parts snapped up and fused together.

They fit like a glove. Not the rigid, unmovable leather that kept you from using your hands properly. They were like lambskin.

"Please." Jamie stood and offered me his hand.

I got up and he led me through the store. Jamie was handsome and knew how to be charming, even if neither Lanai nor I were his type. His thick brown hair flowed in waves and was only lightly peppered with flecks of gray. Few wrinkles dared to settle in his brow. His warm brown eyes and trim physique made him look young.

The shoes caressed my feet. I felt like I was walking on air.

Jamie led me past more mannequins. I wove around the cluster of mannequins, wearing Nationalist Loyalty shirts bearing popular slogans. *Protect the Republic. Conformity is Unity. Loyalty Trumps Freedom. Death to Traitors.*

I was careful not to touch the mannequins for fear their brand of nationalism was contagious.

"Are you in trouble?" I whispered. "I remember, Jamie. Your ponytail and pink sweaters. Before you complied with the conventional style requirements."

"Needs must, Ms. Carter. Election day looms."

A glance up at Jamie betrayed a shadow in his eyes. He patted my hand. "The watchers pay more attention to you than me, my dear."

I wanted to ask what he meant by that, but we were back at the fitting area, where Lania waited.

"Well?" Jamie asked.

"Remarkable. But," I glanced up at my daughter, "what about rain?"

Jamie and Lania shared a look and laughed. "Waterproof. You won't feel a thing," he said.

"But they're all separate pieces."

"It's technoleather. It comes apart and fuses back together seamlessly. Nothing gets through. This is the basic model, but they also come as Climbers."

"Climbers?" I'd seldom gone shoe shopping for years. Lania had promised me miracles, with footwear that would reduce the strain on my body.

Reaching down to tie laces would be a thing of the past.

I couldn't imagine putting on shoes without bending over, but here I was, genuinely impressed, even if they weren't the Pumas, Nikes, and Jimmy Choos from my youth.

"Climbers can be shoes or boots, with or without heels," Jamie said.

"This I have to see."

Jamie showed me how to wriggle my toe to deactivate the shoes. They unraveled as easily as they'd taken shape around when I'd put them on.

He returned the shoes to their box, opened another package and set out a different pair. Again, as soon as my feet were on the insoles, the shoe parts wrapped themselves around me.

A quick tutorial taught me how to activate the shoes.

"You can link them to your EyeScreen and control them with that," Jamie said.

I walked around the fitting area. "They really are remarkable."

"See, Mom?" Lania said.

"I'll take them."

I adjusted to the shoes and AudioBots, which reminded me how many calories were in cheese sticks and how much fat was in chocolate cake.

They were still in the testing phase for elderly Republicans. I could mute them, but they reminded me to take my medication and pay my bills. Even I had to admit they were convenient and I muted them less and less.

However, I set them to silent on election day.

Lania insisted we go near the end of polling, so we left late in the day, whizzing along the old road, past our neighbor's home.

I gasped. Black outfits covered a swarm of armed men bearing black helmets and Kevlar vests with *ICE* displayed. Internment Compliance Enforcement. The Sanders knelt in the middle of the lawn, hands clasped on their heads. Eyes closed.

Lania tsked. "I saw your petition for the wall. It's surprising this didn't happen years ago."

How could she be so casual about it? But the Republic was the only world Lania knew. The hope for the future rested in restoring the true government, forced to flee after the attack on January 6, the start of the second Civil War.

The next generation would heal when individual freedoms were restored. The right to love, marry, choose, think.

How had she seen that petition? I thought about the alleged new boyfriend, her use of the buzzwords.

What didn't I know?

The world became a gray cement and steel blur until we slowed near the Administration Office. A group of convicts in gray and white jumpsuits swept sidewalks and collected trash as armed guards watched them. A convict looked up, exhaust blowing his coiffed hair back. Jamie. I gasped.

When we reached the polling station, I climbed out of the vessel, limbs trembling. We'd waited for years for this election day. And still they rounded up non-conformists whose only crimes were not being molded into the perfect Republican image.

Lania led the way up the steps, laughing and chatting with friends and strangers alike.

She could talk to anyone with ease.

We snaked our way through the armed men. Eventually, uniformed law enforcement officers scanned identity chips in our hands, confirmed our citizenship, and sent us to the booths.

Lania went in and voted first and returned with a smile.

"Hurry, Mom. I have a surprise."

The boyfriend? I stepped inside the booth. The brown wood façade on the outside gave way to steel inside; a touch screen activated, a ray scanned my hand again, and a voice in my head asked me to confirm my identity on the screen.

I tapped my temple. Hadn't I turned the AudioBots off?

We automatically activate for national events.

Unbelievable. I pressed the display, confirming my identity.

There was only one choice in this election. Did I support the current leader or did I support the leader in exile?

Two choices for the future. The Emperor or the rightful winner of the fateful elections all those years ago, though they weren't called that here. The ballot listed the Emperor and the Traitor. To this new order, truth was in the label, not the act; they never called it the coup d'état that it was.

The Emperor lost the election, but his followers started the Second Civil War and eventually unleashed the technical revolution. Bots were in place long before, and every electronic system was vulnerable. He'd declared victory, banished our true leader, and assumed control of the military and government agencies. Eventually, he had buttons to push to maintain his control.

America ended with a whimper and the Republic was born.

Absences followed. Non-conformists, branded socialists, and enemies of the state? Gone.

Dissidents fueled the new for-profit prison system that built roads and sky-high border walls.

My friends disappeared until only those who blended in remained.

Now, a second chance to put things right. I put my mark beside our true leader and confirmed my vote.

A web of pain shot up my legs. The Climbers rose to boot height and the boots' legs rose higher still, until they encased my knees in technoleather.

The material tightened. The boots pushed my toes back toward my heel and forced the sides of my feet to curl. I fumbled with the controls, but the AudioBots sent a long high C slicing through my skull.

"Ahhhgggg." I bent over and clutched my ears with my hands.

What was going on? Another malfunction?

My voting options remained on the screen and a new button appeared.

Press to Change Vote.

Hot tears streaming down my cheeks.

"Like hell." Again, I confirmed my vote.

The leather shot up over my body, right to my throat, squeezing all of the air out of me. *Press to Change Vote* flashed green then red.

I gasped for breath. My body slumped against the display and somehow, the *Press to Change Vote* blinked, taking me back to my original options.

Air flew down my throat and filled my lungs.

From outside, I heard Lania's laughter. I looked at the technoleather, reshaped into my original, wonderful, comfortable shoes.

Choose the candidate you affirm.

That voice in my head again. Not telling me who to vote for, but still issuing a warning.

Constructive limiting.

The language of the government. Explaining why people needed fewer choices instead of more. Indecision had plagued this once-great nation. People were so confused they thought their gender was a choice. Technolution and the Republic had to save people from their own misguided selves.

Only one choice would let me leave the booth alive. I thought of my neighbors, on their knees, surrounded by armed officers. I saw Jamie's face and knew my fate hinged on this vote.

I tapped the box beside the Emperor name, confirmed, wiped my tears, and stepped outside.

Lania led me toward the exit, took my hand and, for the first time, I saw the ring.

How could I have missed it? The stone was bigger than the bed of a fingernail.

"I want you to meet someone."

She took me through a side door.

A man stepped toward us and smiled. My EyeScreen delivered the ID. Eldest son of the Emperor. With brown hair styled like his father's and appropriately white skin.

Waves of nausea rolled over me.

Armed guards stepped forward to open a door behind the happy couple. They led me outside, in front of hundreds of people shadowed in the gathering darkness. People wearing shirts with Loyalist slogans, waving red flags with the Lion Guard emblem, chanting the Emperor's name.

Lania and Jonathan kissed. The crowd cheered. Propagandists moved in with their cameras to secure their shots.

My EyeScreen identified a government official. Georgia Conroy grabbed a microphone and declared the Emperor victorious. From then on, she said, January 6 would be a national holiday.

Reclamation Day.

"The day we took our nation back!"

Conroy turned and her eyes narrowed as she looked at me.

I forced a thin smile and choked back the bile rising in my throat. Fireworks crackled above us, the crowd filled with creamy faces shimmering with red and gold.

A sea of soulless eyes stared into me as my AudioBot reminded me to clap and smile along.

OF TWO MINDS

Marco Etheridge

"Let me get this straight. You're proposing to bring dead troopers back to life?"

The two docs just stand there, dressed in identical white coveralls. They exchange glances, then turn to face the angry officer.

"No, Captain Jenkins, we're proposing to reawaken brain-dead fighters. There is a substantial difference."

Captain Robert Jenkins pinches the bridge of his nose hard enough to hurt. The pain is tangible, a verifiable reality, as opposed to the insanity of the current situation.

A single company of provisional infantry to defend the entire colony of Sector Seven. Nine hundred civilian colonists and only four platoons of grunts to protect them. One hundred and ten soldiers counting himself. And fifty-seven of those grunts have been turned into brainless vegetables.

Sector Seven, a lonely colonial outpost on a barren asteroid. No one gave two shits about Sector Seven. A cold rock that isn't worth the trouble of a foreign patrol, much less an attack. But that was before Earth got wiped out. Then the Luna colonies went dark. For all Jenkins knows, he commands the last existing company of the Colonial Armed Forces in the entire solar system.

The attackers had swept in from the deep shadows of space, without warning or mercy. Earth gone in four months, then Luna in six. The colonists and soldiers of Sector Seven were marooned in the asteroid belt.

At first, the situation was critical. Then it got worse. After two months of isolation, the Krang landed. They came on a single scout ship, forced to this lonely rock by the same marauders that wiped out the rest of the solar system.

Captain Jenkins figures the Krang want what the colonists had: food, water, and shelter. A place to hide. Sector Seven was no longer marooned. It was besieged.

"Captain?"

"Excuse me, Doctors. Just assessing our position. You were saying?"

"We would like to test this procedure on one of the casualties. As you know better than anyone, time is critical. We can't send out a request for reinforcements. Sector Seven is on its own."

"I'm fully aware of our tactical situation."

"Then you agree to a trial run?"

"We're not exactly wading in options. Okay, run it by me again."

The medicos look more at ease now, safe in their medical element.

"Normally, we would implant the device internally, wrapping it around the reptilian brain stem. The device functions as a surrogate operating system, a brain reboot. The implanted system takes over all functions of the host body, including cognition. Since our medical tech is limited, we'll have to go with an external mount, just at the spot where the nape meets the skull."

"We bolt a new brain onto a brain-dead soldier. Do I have that right?"

"In layman's terms, yes. We've programmed the device to have a complete knowledge of soldiering. Of course, there will be a period of adjustment, but we estimate no more than forty-eight hours."

"And then I get, what? A veteran or a raw recruit?"

"We believe the subject will be fully combat-ready."

"What happens to the, what is the word I'm looking for? The personality of the soldier before the Krang zapped him. What happens to that?"

"Gone, I'm afraid. Overwritten. But it's already gone. We don't fully understand what type of weapon the Krang are using, but it appears to erase the consciousness of their victims, hence the vegetative state."

"So, broke is broke, as they say. I don't see that we have much choice. Proceed."

"Captain, do you have a preferred subject for the first trial?"

This, at least, is an easy question.

"Yes, Sergeant Jake Pierce. Jocko Pierce. Best soldier we've got. Or had. Keep me posted."

Jenkins turns on his heel and exits the sickbay, glad for the swish-lock of the auto door. He hates hospitals, hates docs. Always had. Now, with half his troops laid out like zombies, he loathes the white-coated bastards.

The captain stalks down a cramped subterranean corridor carved into the asteroid's bedrock. The rough walls and arched ceiling are whitewashed to reflect the glow lights. He turns into a side corridor, then stops before an auto-lock. A stenciled sign above the door reads: Provisional Infantry, Sector Seven, First Company. There is no second company.

Waiting for the retinal scan, Jenkins' face is grim. The door pulses open, and he steps through. Operations for ProvIF S7/1 are contained in a low-arched room. Equipment racks line the rock. The armory occupies the next chamber.

Three desks are crammed against the back wall. Not much privacy or privilege of rank on Sector Seven.

Jenkins crosses the room and slumps into a chair behind one of the desks. The other two are empty. His Number Two and First Sergeant wouldn't be needing their workstations. Both are laid out on gurneys, comatose as cabbages. Captain Jenkins is on his own.

Alone, staring down at the meaningless clutter that litters his desk, the hard set of the captain's jaw disappears. He feels like bawling.

Fucking Krang. He wasn't trained for this shit. He's more policeman than soldier. His orders were to enforce tariff laws and curtail smuggling. No smuggling now, not with Earth and Luna gone black and silent. And no one left to send new orders.

How do you fight space monkeys who vanished like rabbits, then reappeared behind you and smacked you with a brain-killing club? It wasn't fair.

It was the grunts who coined the name, the lucky ones who came back from the first fight. If you could call that debacle a fight. The little alien bastards had some sort of personal cloaking device, a technology far beyond the standard weapons issued to the Colonial Infantry. Despite their sneaky cloaking, or maybe because of it, the Krang fought with sticks.

The survivors called them Krang sticks. Krang! That's what a near miss sounded like crashing past your combat helmet. Closer than that, who knows what the sound was. Ask one of the senseless bastards who got slammed. Maybe they know. But they're not talking.

Two missions to push the Krang back into space where they belonged. Both missions total disasters. Half his grunts were down and not a single dead Krang to tally against those losses.

All his best fighters were laid out in sickbay. The pint-sized Krang tagged Lieutenant Gregg in the first melee. They got First Sergeant Jake Pierce in the second. Jocko Pierce, Top, the guy who really ran the outfit. Without Jocko's lead, the surviving grunts are nervous as sheep. Captain Jenkins feels scared and useless.

Now the docs are trying to pull off a miracle. And barring a miracle, ProvIF S7/1 is doomed, and the rest of Sector Seven as well.

Captain Jenkins drops his head into his hands.

Everything is black. He tries to move, tries to blink his eyes. Nothing happens. Less than nothing. He has no sensation, no sense of up or down, no pull of gravity. No pain.

Get your shit together, soldier!

Sergeant Jake Pierce hears the words in his head, but the darkness is silent. You gotta move, Jocko. Get your men and get them out of here. Focus, for fucksake. You're the guy in charge. The boys are counting on you.

Then Jocko Pierce sees a grey glow, a faint glimmer on the far horizon of the blackness that engulfs him. The dim light rolls out of his vision, then reappears, again and again, and each time the glow seems closer. Like he's tumbling through space, untethered and adrift, pulled toward some distant nebula.

Now the light rushes at him and the darkness vanishes, replaced by a scene viewed as if through a porthole. Shit, he's in sickbay. Right, okay, get a grip on yourself. Sickbay is better than a body bag. You got tagged, but the boys brought you back.

The room resolves itself into rows of gurneys, with bodies laid out on each. Jocko tries to scan the scene, but his eyes do not respond.

Look left. Nothing. Look right. No response. Left eye, blink. Still nothing. Jocko's mind signals fear, but there is no corresponding tightening of muscles, no metallic taste of adrenaline at the back of his tongue. He is devoid of sensation.

Paralyzed, that had to be it. But what about his eyes? Then his field of vision shifts, panning upward like a movie camera on a gantry. He sees his feet at the end of the gurney. His body sitting up now, but how? He wills his right foot to move. Nothing happens. So not paralyzed, but not in control. Then it hits him. If he wasn't controlling his muscles, who was?

Excuse me. Who are you?

A voice slamming into his mind, a voice he did not recognize. A stranger in his head. What the hell was happening?

You are not supposed to be here.

Right, and fuck you too, asshole.

You should know that I hear the thoughts you formulate.

Right. Okay then, who are you and what are you doing to me? Is this a drug reaction, some crazy shit the docs dosed me with?

Before we go further, am I correct in assuming that you are First Sergeant Jake Pierce?

Yeah, duh, Jocko Pierce. That's me. Who the hell are you?

This is perplexing. Please allow me a few moments to process this information.

Process what? It's a simple question. Who the hell are you and what did those stupid medics do to me?

Silence.

Then the vision shifts. Jocko's body swings its legs off the bed. His feet must hit the floor, but he feels nothing. His body is a robot over which he has no control. All he can do is watch, a parasite along for the ride.

A hand, his hand, reaching for a glass of water. The water coming closer, tilting, then disappearing out of sight. No sensation of swallowing, or of a long thirst being quenched, nothing.

Then the goddamn voice again.

I apologize for the delay, Sergeant Pierce. It appears we have a slight malfunction. A glitch.

You think? I wake up in sickbay with voices in my head and no control over my body. Yeah, I think that qualifies as a glitch.

Please remain calm. Your brain functions were determined to be zero. That was the medical assessment, not mine. I was installed as an alternative operating system so that your body could be returned to active duty.

You were installed? Who the hell are you? No, wait. What the hell are you?

I am a programmed human operating system. I have taken over your body's functions.

I have a suggestion. Get the fuck out of my head, uninstall yourself, and give me back my body. Like, right now!

Very well. There, I am not at present controlling any of your body's functions.

Jocko's slice of vision goes black, like his eyelids are sliding shut, which they are. Open your eyes, Jocko. Open your goddamn eyes, man!

Nothing. He feels nothing, controls nothing. He's a puppeteer without a puppet. Dead, but not dead.

Okay, I get your point. And you can't give me back my body?

I'm afraid that's impossible, Sergeant Pierce. You have suffered severe brain trauma. Can you recall any memories?

Maybe, if you shut up and let me think.

What was the last thing he remembered? Fuzzy, broken images, like trying to look through cotton candy.

Okay, right, first there was the contact. An unidentified ship landed, no protocol, intentions unknown. Lieutenant Gregg takes the first patrol. Reconnoiter, ascertain whether friendly or hostile, establish contact if friendly, do not engage if hostile. By the numbers. Only that's not how it went.

What really happened?

Stop that, it's annoying as hell.

Sorry. Please continue.

Gregg has First and Third Platoon loaded aboard four gun carriers. Takes them right to the coordinates. No sign of a ship. No sign of anything. The Lieutenant decides to do a sweep on foot, him and First Platoon, with Third standing backup. That's when things went to shit.

I was at base, listening to the feed from the comm station. One minute everything is by the numbers, and the next it's chaos. First Platoon is under attack. Third Platoon is talking crazy, little hostiles beating our guys with sticks. They can't lay down backup fire because it's a melee.

Nothing made sense, the captain shouting 'Disengage, disengage!' and then the comms go dead.

Three minutes, max, I've got Second and Fourth Platoons firing up the gun carriers and strapping in. Then Third is back on the comms. Retreating to base with wounded, twenty-five soldiers down, the entire foot patrol taken out except for two grunts. No fatalities.

Things didn't get a lot clearer when the patrol limped back to base. We carted in the wounded until sickbay was almost full. Didn't know then how crowded it was going to get. Then the docs started wrestling the casualties out of their suits, and things got weirder.

We finally get First Platoon laid out on gurneys but couldn't find a single wound on any of them. Their body armor is intact, suits not breached. But every soldier, woman or man, has been knocked into a coma. None of them show any signs of waking up.

I debriefed the two survivors from First, Gates and Graves. She covers his back, and he's got hers. Bad asses, the both of them, but their report makes no sense.

Gates said the hostiles were small, no more than four feet tall. Said the bastards appeared out of thin air, swinging clubs. One almost got her. Said it sounded like a cracked bell ringing in her ears. Krang! Then the hostile was gone—Poof! Graves just nodded his head, like always. That boy hardly talks.

I ask him did they get any and he shrugs. Maybe one or two, Top. Gates talking then, saying Graves tagged two of them. Said the hostiles went up like white flares. But there was no time to check it out, Top. That shit was intense. Krang-Krang-Krang, the whole platoon dropping like rocks. Then everything went quiet. The little fuckers just vanished.

Logging my report, I'm seeing how nuts it looks. Hostiles in black body armor, black helmets, no bigger than human kids, but swinging for the fences. Graves hardly talks, but he did say the Krang were fast, quick as cats. Humanoid, wide shoulders, thick legs. I read it back, shaking my head. Sawed off humanoids armed with clubs beating the shit out of a heavily-armed platoon of Colonial AF.

Twenty-four years I've been soldiering. Turned forty-two last earth year. An old man to troopers like Gates and Graves. I maybe spent two years earth-side that whole twenty-four. Seen some weird shit out here, but this took the cake. Weird or not, I logged it in like any other action.

Twelve hours later, I rolled out with the entire company, the gun carriers loaded with everything they could carry. The only ones left at base were the comms corporal and the captain. Last place you want Number One is anywhere near a fight.

Might as well have packed slingshots. We got our asses handed to us. I took the gun carriers within a thousand meters of the landing coordinates, but there was nothing. Either our data was wrong, or the hostiles were invisible.

Then I made the same mistake Gregg made. I took the troops out of the carriers. I wanted evidence, footprints, discarded weapons, anything to give me an edge. Instead, I walked those soldiers into a fight we couldn't win. Stupid.

We went in ready and armed for bear. Four squads, two-by-two, half with pulse guns, half with projectile carbines. Everyone locked and loaded.

Everything was by the numbers. I pulled up short of the scene of the first fight, fanned the squads out into an arc. I signaled move and the squads advanced. Textbook maneuver, for all the good it did.

Ten seconds later, all hell broke loose. Hostiles materialized out of thin air. For a split second, I saw a shimmer, like heat waves dancing over an air vent. Then one of the bastards was right in front of me, swinging a long club. I dodged left and the club just missed my helmet. Krang! I popped off two quick rounds as the krang vanished. I doubt I hit him. Or her. Or it.

There was no line. The Krang were everywhere, behind us, in front, appearing and disappearing right in the middle of a squad. I saw my soldiers going down left and right. Couldn't lay down effective fire without hitting the trooper next to you.

The comms were a tangle of shouted warnings and the echo of Krang–Krang. A shout crackled over the headset. Top, your six!

I swung one-eighty, leading with my carbine. The last thing I saw was the end of that little bastard's club. Then nothing.

And now you are back from nothing.

Shit, that's going to take some getting used to.

I am sorry, Sergeant Pierce. I did not mean to startle you.

Look, if we're going to be crammed in here, I think we can dispense with rank. Call me Jocko.

Very well, if you insist.

I do insist. And what the hell do I call you? You got a name?

I am IHRS-Zed-392. Interactive Human Replacement System.

Okay, that's not going to work. You need a name. How about Gizmo?

Gizmo, yes, I like that name. It is humorous.

You have a sense of humor?

I do. I am programmed in many aspects of human behavior. Would you care to hear a joke? Three men walk into a spaceport...

Whoa, Gizmo. Another time, maybe.

I apologize. You are correct, Jocko. There are important matters to attend to. It interests me that your consciousness has returned. This is not the case with any of the other soldiers. And there are portions of your narrative that may be of great use to us.

Such as? I'm all ears.

I don't understand.

See? We need to work on your humor skills. It means I'm listening. What's useful besides that the Krang kicked my ass?

Yes, it is evident that the Krang, as you call them, won the battle. Yet it is the method by which they achieved their victory that may hold the key.

Meaning?

None of your soldiers were killed. I would venture the theory that they were incapacitated. The Krang do not seem disposed to eliminate their enemies, but to best them. This ritualized form of combat has precedents among some of the aboriginal peoples from your home planet.

Holy shit, Gizmo, I see what you're getting at. Counting coup, like some of the ancient Native American tribes. I've read about them, the Cheyenne, the Crow.

Exactly, Jocko. Also the Sioux, Blackfoot, and others.

That's probably something they teach at the academy.

What academy are you referring to?

The Officers Academy, where green officers learn how to get their troops killed.

Why would that be a subject for study? And why would the officers be green?

Forget it, Gizmo. If we're on the right track with this coup thing, then each side has two completely different objectives. We want to force the Krang off Sector Seven. The Krang want to demonstrate their bravery. Shit, we're going at this all wrong.

I believe that may be the case, Jocko. I am recalling a quote that seems applicable to our current situation: Success in warfare is gained by carefully accommodating ourselves to the enemy's purpose.

The Art of War. I've carried old Sun Tzu with me since I was a corporal. Okay, Gizmo, time to come up with a new plan.

For Jocko Pierce, it's like viewing a scene on a movie screen. Gizmo is controlling everything, doing all the talking. Jocko is staring out of a porthole. On the other side of the goddamned porthole, another man is staring back at him. At them.

Staff Sergeant Bronski looks confused. Hell, the poor bastard has a right to be. Bronski is the company's armorer, a tech guy, not the sort of man who is used to seeing ghosts. And standing in front of him is First Sergeant Pierce, newly back from the dead. Worse, Top doesn't sound right. It's like there's some other voice coming out of his mouth.

"Top, with all due respect, you sure you should be out of sickbay? You don't seem like yourself."

Psst... Gizmo, you're freaking Bronski out. You gotta talk normal, more like me. Blame it on the implant or something.

I will try, Jocko.

Jocko hears Gizmo clear his throat. He wishes he could feel it, could feel anything.

"The doctors cleared me, Sergeant Bronski. It will take time to get used to this new implant. Please bear with me."

Loosen up, Gizmo. Try swearing.

"Fuck. I mean, fuck sickbay. We have work to do."

Okay, better. Now let's get Bronski on board with this.

"You understand what we need, Sergeant Bronski?"

What they need is a bang stick, a fighting club that packs a thunder punch. A pugil stick mated with the cartridge from a pulse rifle. They want Bronski to build it and build it fast.

"I got it, Top. Mount a pulse cartridge on the body of a pugil stick and build a contact trigger on the business end. The tech is primitive, no problem. But I gotta warn you, this thing is going to kick like a mule."

"That is a risk we will have to accept."

Don't forget the decorations.

"One more thing, Sergeant. We need to ornament the weapon."

"We?"

"Affirmative. We, as in a team. You and I."

"You want me to make the thing pretty?"

"Not pretty, Bronski. Think ritualistic. Tribal. Put some damn feathers on it, rawhide, that sort of thing."

"Okay, Top, whatever you say. I'll get on it."

Bronski's face disappears from Jocko's view as Gizmo turns their body and walks out of the armory.

He thinks we're nuts, Gizmo.

Quite possibly, but will he do it?

He'll do it alright. Bronski's the best. The question is, do we really want him to? If he builds it, we might be stupid enough to use the damn thing. C'mon, let's go next door and brief the captain.

They find Captain Jenkins at his desk, head in his hands as if he hasn't moved in hours. Perhaps he hasn't. The captain looks up, sees First Sergeant Pierce, and then he's blinking like an owl. Pushes himself up like he's the one who should be saluting.

Gizmo throws off a sharp salute, way too formal for the captain. Jocko sees the confusion on the poor bastard's face, then relief.

"Top! Damn docs didn't tell me you were out of sickbay. How are you feeling?"

"I feel fine, Sir. Thank you for asking. I am ready to get to work."

Captain Jenkins tilts his head.

"Are you sure you're okay, Sergeant? You sound funny."

Now you've done it, Gizmo. Jenkins is just a piddling captain. You're treating him like a general or something.

Sorry, Jocko. But protocol is an important part of...

Damn protocol. Tell him about the mission. Don't ask him. Tell him. And loosen up, okay?

Gizmo does his best. Now he's only about a half-kilometer short of the real Jocko Pierce. Still, he manages to curse once or twice, even if he sounds like a schoolboy dropping his first f-bomb.

Once he hears the mission, Jenkins flops back in his chair, a stunned look smeared across his face.

"Top, I know you've got way more combat hours than I do, but this is a crazy idea. You want to go out with a single gun carrier? No ground support? Sounds like suicide to me."

"No Sir. I need a closer look at the Krang position. A first-hand report. No need to jeopardize additional soldiers."

"Okay, Top. You know best. Or you usually do, anyway. But you better not take any unnecessary chances. That's an order. You don't make it back, this unit falls apart."

Jocko Pierce sits alone in the bay of the gun carrier. Alone with Gizmo. The troop bay seems cavernous without a full platoon aboard. The pilot and Graves are sealed off up front. Gates is in the firing turret.

On a digital display, Jocko sees the stark terrain of Sector Seven floating past, exactly what the pilot is seeing. The carrier is floating over the desolate waste, two meters off the deck, drawing close to the coordinates where the Krang ship should be, but isn't.

Jocko leans forward, monitoring a position readout, comparing the bearings to the video feed.

Okay, Gizmo. Just like we planned it. The comm line crackles to life.

"Two hundred meters. Bring us down to a crawl."

Inertia drags forward as the carrier slows.

"One hundred more, then bring us down facing on our current bearing."

The ship slows again.

"How's this, Top?"

"Good. Set us down here. Gates, you okay up there?"

A female voice fills the headset.

"All good, Top. Firing systems hot."

This is the tough part, Gizmo. They aren't going to like this, so you've got to sell it.

I will do my best, Jocko.

"Right. Listen up, you three. Straight ahead, five hundred meters, you see that rock outcropping?"

Three affirmatives.

"Look just past it. You see where the horizon is distorted, like a faint heat signature?"

Affirmations again, but less certain.

"Graves, you're navigating, so you track targets for Gates. That big shimmer on the horizon is the Krang ship. That's your target number two. Target number one is the area in front of that rock, where the patrols got into trouble. Target one, target two. Clear?"

"Got it, Top."

"Roger, Top."

"Good. Here's the operation. I'm going out on a solo reconnoiter. If the Krang take me down, you light up target one with AP fire, pulse and projectile both. Do you understand?"

"But Top..."

"No buts. You do it. Fire for effect, full bore. Take down any and all individual Krang fighters. Then you switch to target two. Throw the heavy stuff at their ship. Hard projectiles, ion cannon, everything. Keep firing until you've got nothing left, then get the hell out of here. Understood?"

The comm line stays silent for a long moment.

"Understood, Top. I will light those fuckers up."

"Atta girl."

Jocko watches as Gizmo slides the helmet over their head and locks it in place. The face shield display blinks twice in the upper left field of vision, then begins scrolling data.

Are you ready, Jocko?

Born ready, Gizmo. Let's take our big stick and go for a walk.

Gizmo taps the comm line.

"Secured for exterior. Open bay door."

Coup stick over their shoulder, they climb down the dropped ramp and step onto the rocky surface of Sector Seven.

Seems a lot further than half a kilometer.

Interesting. My perception is similar.

We've still got time. I could talk you out of this. Or you could talk me out of it. Either way.

But you don't wish to be talked out of it, Jocko.

On the money. Just talking trash while there's still time to talk.

The gyro-grav boots keep their feet in contact with the surface. Gizmo walks them forward, his footsteps lighter and faster than they would be on Earth. He carries the coup stick at port arms, business tip up. Two bands of plastic feathers, Bronski's fabricated decorations, dance from the shaft of the weapon.

Okay, we're getting close. Look sharp, or someone's going to wind up dead.

True, but you've already been dead once.

That is some cold comfort, Gizmo. If I had a body, I'd be laughing.

Jocko peers forward. He sees the disturbed surface, confused footprints in the dust. This is where the fight took place. What's left of his disjointed memory flashes an image, clear and certain.

Hey, I just remembered something. The Krang. I think all of them are right-handed. And I'm left-handed. Or was.

You are still left-handed. That information may prove useful.

Look sharp. This is the spot. They're here. I can feel it. Keep your eyes peeled. I hope this old body works for you.

Gizmo does not reply. Jocko sees his arms extend, brandishing the coup stick. One foot forward, body slipping into a crouch. Ready or not, here we go.

There's a smear of motion across the air in front of them, like a clear film distorting in a non-existent wind. In the next split second, a single Krang appears.

For one frozen instant, Jocko sees a helmeted and black-suited warrior, weapon held high and ready. The Krang's face plate is mirrored. A reflection hovers in the mirror, a tiny man holding a ridiculous stick. Jocko realizes he is staring at himself. Then everything dissolves into a blur of motion as the fight begins.

The Krang swings from his right, hard and fast, low to high. Jocko hears air sizzling, but it's all in his disembodied head. There is no sound, no atmosphere to transmit it. Gizmo pivots left with their coup stick held vertical, hands wide. The stick blocks the Krang's swing. The physical shock of the impact is very real.

Snake-quick, the Krang spins away, pirouetting like a Luna Gei-Han dancer. Now he stabs in from his weak side, using the Krang stick like a spear. The tip is a blur, a missile streaking into their face shield. Then the Gizmo is crouching and swinging, parrying the lunge from below and sending the Krang's thrust high.

Momentum brings the little bastard in close. Gizmo pivots to throw a left knee into the Krang. Jocko watches the horizon dip and swirl with each move. It's like being trapped inside an out-of-control flight simulator.

The knee kick drives the Krang back, but the blow is not enough to knock their enemy down. The Krang extends its arms high and left, holding the Krang stick aloft as if for an overhand strike.

It's a feint, Gizmo!

I see it.

Instead of striking down, their half-size foe twirls the Krang stick behind its head, coming around with a viscous arc knee-high to the rocky ground.

Gizmo jabs the coup stick into the ground like he's planting a colonial flag. The Krang stick stops dead, then rebounds. For a single heartbeat, the Krang is off balance. Gizmo lunges forward with the butt end of the coup stick. A fountain of dust follows the lunge, particles glistening in the harsh light.

The coup stick stabs into the middle of the Krang's chest, driving it back two full steps.

Good shot, Gizmo!

Yes, Jocko, but the fight is not done.

As if to prove Gizmo's words, the Krang is back in a fighting crouch, Krang stick held at port arms. Then Jocko sees a shimmer pass between them and their enemy. He remembers the last fight.

He's going invisible. Behind, Gizmo, he's gonna come from behind!

The shimmer turned to a swirl and the Krang vanished. Instead of turning around, Gizmo runs straight toward the spot where the Krang disappeared. As he dashes forward, the Krang reappears, weapon held high. Krang stick smashes down on the space they just vacated. Gizmo swings around to face the befuddled enemy.

That fucked him up!

Yes, thanks to your warning, Jocko.

Watch the little shit. He's going to try something sneaky.

The Krang edged sideways, circling, and they circled with him. Their gyro-grav boots kicked up miniature volcanoes of dust. Without warning, the Krang lurches sideways, as if tripping over some hidden rock.

Gizmo feints a half-step forward then pushes back as the enemy swing comes out of nowhere. The Krang is not off balance, not stumbling. He's swinging for the fences. Krang! The business end of the Krang stick misses their face shield by mere centimeters. The shock wave jars their helmet.

The Krang allows the missed stroke to spin itself back into a fighting stance

Our enemy uses a classic swordsman's feint, Jocko.

I told you the fucker was sneaky.

Deception takes many forms.

Gizmo raises the coup stick high and left. Jock sees the pulse cartridge below their hands. Gizmo is using the wrong end! Before Jocko can shout a warning. Gizmo swings the butt end of the stick down, but the blow is slow and awkward. The

Krang raises his weapon at the horizontal, an easy block to Gizmo's feeble blow.

Gizmo does not strike. He drops to their knees, pulling their arms down to chest level, then flinging them forward, as if casting a spell. But it's not spells Gizmo is throwing. The coup stick spears forward, pulse cartridge first, passing under the Krang's misdirected block. The weapon slams into the Krang's mirrored face shield, the detonator triggers the pulse cartridge, and a burst of white engulfs both warriors.

The explosion of electric white fades to complete blackness. Jocko Pierce is suspended in time. One split second, or maybe an hour, a year. Then a bleak spacescape blurs into focus, the rocky surface of Sector Seven. And a few meters away, sprawled on its back in the dust, lies the fallen Krang.

Jocko tries to make sense of what he's seeing. They seem to have fallen to one knee, maybe staggered by the pulse blast. He tries to stand, remembers that he can't, then remembers a whole lot of stuff he wishes he could forget.

Gizmo, you still there?

I believe so, Jocko. I'm a bit shaken. The pulse shock had a significant impact.

I'll say. You knocked that little fucker for a loop. Down, but not dead. Look, he's moving.

The Krang *was* moving. The black-suited warrior rolls onto all fours, then pushes itself to its feet. It staggers a step or two, helmet swinging from side to side. Then it crouches to the ground. When their opponent stands up, it's holding the Krang stick.

Shit, Gizmo, we don't have another pulse cartridge. We fired our only shot.

We may not need another. Let us wait and see.

They do not wait long. The Krang turns to face them, arms extended. Its weapon rests across open palms. Jocko gets his first good look at the Krang's hands. They are lean and long, with opposable thumbs and three slender fingers each.

The two warriors stand a few meters apart, still as statues.

Then the Krang does something Jocko could never have imagined. It bows. Their enemy bends forward at the waist, holding its weapon out as it bows. One heartbeat, two, and the Krang straightens itself and stands rock still.

Before Jocko can react, Gizmo replicates the Krang's gesture, executing a perfect formal bow, holding it for the correct interval, then straightening back to standing.

What do you suppose happens now, Jocko?

I have no idea. None whatsoever.

As if sensing the question, the Krang tilts his weapon and plants it on the dusty surface, holding it with one arm extended, just like a recruit learning drills.

The little bastard knows parade rest.

So it would seem, Jocko.

The Krang raises its empty hand and executes a twirling gesture. The empty space shimmers across a wide semicircle and a dozen Krang appear. Another hand gesture and all thirteen Krang sink to the dust, legs crossing gracefully beneath them, Krang sticks across their laps.

And now, Jocko?

Same as them, Gizmo. Our guy is in command. Looks like we're going to have a parley.

Gizmo lowers their body to the ground, what's left of the coup stick balanced across their folded knees.

Alright, before we parley, let's make sure Gates doesn't vaporize the lot of us. Open all comm channels and tell them to hold their fire.

Gizmo activates a control and static hiss fills their battle helmet.

"Gun Carrier One, do you copy?"

"Copy, Top."

"Gun Carrier One, we are engaging in negotiations. Hold your fire, repeat, hold your fire. Copy?"

"Affirmative, Top. Copy. Standing by."

Okay, Gizmo. Let's see if these munchkins will talk to us. Give 'em the peace hand.

Gizmo holds up one hand, palm out. The Krang leader responds with the same gesture.

Then the static hiss crackles into a series of what sounds like guttural yowls. The Krang is speaking, but the Auto-Translate yields nothing.

Right. It seems were done fighting, but we can't talk with them. Now what?

I suggest sign language, Jocko.

Give it your best shot. Try to find out why they're here, maybe what they want.

Gizmo raises a hand to their helmet, taps it, then shakes their head. He holds both hands out, palms up. A question. Then he points to the shimmering aura beyond the rock outcropping. The Krang looks to where he is pointing. Then Gizmo holds both hands forward as if holding an imaginary stick. He mimics breaking the stick, then repeats the question gesture.

A long moment. Nothing. Then the Krang nods once. More yowling fills their helmet, but the Krang leader has turned to his troops. Three of the Krang rise as one and scamper off toward the rock outcropping. The Krang leader turns back to face them, both hands raised palms out. Wait.

Jocko laughs his silent laugh. They don't teach this shit in the manual, Gizmo. We're playing space charades with a bunch of hostile aliens.

It appears so, Jocko. We can only hope they are familiar with the concept.

The wait seems interminable, but it does not last forever. Just when Jocko is sure he cannot endure one more second, he sees the three Krang reappear. The small figures scramble down the rocky slope and trot toward the waiting group. One of them cradles something in its arms.

The three Krang reenter the half circle, stopping before their seated commander. The Krang bearing the object holds the thing out to the leader. He nods once, then flips a hand to indicate Jocko and Gizmo.

The Krang soldier approaches, drops to one knee, and holds out the object. Jocko tries to get a good look at the thing as Gizmo takes it from the Krang's outstretched hands. As soon as Gizmo has possession, the Krang soldier retreats to his place in the half circle and sits down.

Gizmo, if I had to guess, I'd say that's some sort of fuel jet, an atomizer, or valve of some kind.

I concur, Jocko. And it has obviously malfunctioned. There is a large fracture in the housing as well as evidence of burning.

Son of a bitch. These poor bastards aren't invading Sector Seven. They're broke down. Shit, I bet the machinists can duplicate this thing. It doesn't look that complicated.

No, it doesn't. Replicating this part would perhaps kill two birds with one stone as the saying goes.

Right. We make peace and we get the Krang on their way and off Sector Seven. Tell them we can do it.

Gizmo and Jocko climb up the drop ramp and into the gun carrier. The Krang commander follows, leading four of its warriors. One of the soldiers carries the failed fuel apparatus. The Krang sit on the troop bench opposite Gizmo and Jocko.

Let's get some atmo in here. Time to show our faces. Sorry, our face.

Gizmo taps the comm line.

"Secure bay door. Pressurize interior."

"Roger, Top."

The door bolts click into place and lock. A hissing noise fills the troop bay.

"Pressurized, Top. You're good to unseal."

Gizmo ratchets the safety lock on their battle helmet and releases the seal. Jocko imagines the relief of that first breath of atmo, but it's only a memory. He doesn't breathe anymore. The helmet lifts clear of their head, giving the Krang their first look at a human face. Jocko hopes the little bastards don't freak out.

If they have any plans for freaking out, the Krang don't show it. The commander gestures to one of his cadre, who pulls a device from a sealed pocket. The Krang soldier holds the device up, activates it, and waits. The thing emits a soft whirr, a few beeps, then goes silent. The soldier nods and holds the sensor out to its commander. He reads the instrument's display and reaches for his helmet.

If there was going to be any freaking out, it was Jocko's turn. The helmets come off one by one. The Krang not only yowl like felines, but they also look the part. Jocko sees long, flat noses, pointed ears, almond-shaped eyes, and furry faces. The color and pattern of the facial fur vary. The commander's face is a striped grey. Two soldiers resemble orange tomcats. Of the remains pair, one is jet black, and its comrade is white.

Their eyes range from golden yellow to chocolate brown. Studious, serious, observant eyes, and all of them looking at Sergeant Jocko Pierce.

I believe a greeting of some sort is in order.

Yeah, go formal, Gizmo. Pretend you're in a Gei-Han Salon on Luna.

Not something I've experienced, Jocko, but I know the protocol.

Gizmo holds out their forearms, palms up as if offering a sword. Or a coup stick. Still sitting on the crew bench, he bows at the waist, forty-five degrees, holds the posture, then straightens their body.

The Krang commander nods. Some quick soft yowls pass between the Krang. Jocko figures it's the equivalent of feline whispering. Then all five of the alien warriors hold out their three-fingered hands and bow in unison.

A long silence follows. The Krang look at them, and they look at the Krang. The air crackles with tension. There is no hostility, but no one is relaxing either.

The comm line breaks the quiet.

"Ten minutes out, Top."

The Krang commander cocks its head. Gizmo holds up their hands, fingers and thumbs out. Then he spins one forefinger in the air and points to the sensor unit strapped to their wrist. The commander observes these gestures, nods, yowl-whispers to his crew.

You think the Krang got that?

I have no idea, Jocko. At least they do not appear to be insulted.

The captain is going to shit when he meets this bunch. I'm kinda looking forward to that.

Captain Jenkins does almost shit when he sees the Krang. The alien guests cause quite a stir inside the Sector Seven compound. Most of the civilians are better behaved than the captain. Gates and Graves act as rear escorts.

The machinist foreman seems to hit it off with one of the Krang soldiers. Human machinist and alien solider pass the burnt-out fuel part back and forth. A few gestures, some quick sketches, and the pair are suddenly thick as thieves. Without a word or a yowl, they vanish into the depths of the machine shop.

The Krang commander seems to take this in stride. Ignoring his missing soldier, the Krang boss turns to Captain Jenkins, who is at a loss. Jocko urges Gizmo to the rescue.

"Captain, let's take them to sickbay. Maybe they can give us a clue about our wounded."

"Good thinking, Top."

"Graves, let the docs know we're on our way."

"Roger, Top."

Sergeant Pierce leads Captain Jenkins out of the machine shop, and Jenkins pretends to lead the Krang guests. They follow rock-hewn corridors, turning left and right, with Gates and Graves marching in step behind them.

The sickbay doors are open, the doctors waiting just inside. If the medicos are freaking out over the Krang, they're hiding it well. The entourage comes to a halt. Fifty-seven gurneys fill the space, each holding a comatose colonial soldier.

What now, Jocko?

Now we see how badly the Krang want their spare parts. Wave them forward and let's see what happens.

Gizmo turns to the Krang commander, then gestures to the fallen colonial troops. The commander looks across the rows of gurneys, then motions to his three soldiers. A low yowling, then he touches each of their furry foreheads. The three Krang soldiers step forward, their Krang sticks held like staffs.

"Top, are you sure we should..."

Gizmo gets a hand up faster than Jocko can warn him. The Krang commander watches every move.

"Captain, I believe the Krang mean well."

Way to go, Gizmo. Better keep an eye on Gates and Graves. We don't want a firefight in sickbay.

Gizmo turns and gives the two fighters a look, flashes them the palm down sign. Be cool. Jocko sees his pit bulls relax, at least a little.

The three Krang move along the narrow aisle and stop at the first gurneys. They raise their Krang sticks and hold them over the foreheads of three wounded soldiers.

Jocko catches movement out of the corner of their eye. Graves is raising his weapon but Gizmo waves him off. The Krang commander half-turns. Gizmo meets its eye, nods. The commander gives a low yowl and the three outstretched Krang sticks glow and pulse, once, twice. The soldiers raise their sticks and move on to the next trio of gurneys. The docs hurry after them, checking the sensor readings.

"Captain, heartbeat increasing, and we've got brain activity. I think the patient is responding."

"Same here, Captain."

"Are they conscious?"

"No, Captain, not conscious. But not comatose, either."

The Krang continue around the gurneys, lighting up the fallen three-by-three. The doctors scurry after them, reading sensors and comparing notes.

The Krang commander watches his soldiers and Jocko Pierce watches the commander. The Krang soldiers reach the last two wounded colonials. The Krang commander yowls and his soldiers pass the remaining two gurneys and return to their leader.

Jocko looks at the last gurney. He recognizes the blank face of Corporal Benson, a decent enough soldier. Then Benson's face blurs. The overhead lights seem to pulse and dim. He hears the captain's voice, angry and loud.

"Why are they stopping? What about those two?"

Gizmo, I don't feel too good. You gotta stop the captain. He'll screw us all for sure.

Jocko sees the Krang leader, sees Gizmo raise a questioning hand. The Krang shakes his head, holds up two fingers, points to himself, points to them. The message is clear. Two of ours, two of yours. We lost and you lost.

"Captain, we have to let this go. The Krang lost two of theirs, so we lose two of ours."

Jocko can't hear the captain's answer. The lights are pulsing faster now. It's like being drunk. Jocko wishes he was drunk. Wishes he was anything. Then he hears Gizmo.

Jocko, what's happening to you? Can you hear me? I'm losing you. Okay, hold on, I'm shutting this down. Try to hang on, Jocko. Just hang on, you hear me?

There's the ceiling. He must have fallen down. Jocko stares up at the lights, the pulsing lights. Who's turning them on and off like that? And faces, faces leaning over him. Doctors, and doctors that look like cats. Cat doctors. Gates and Graves, and that worthless captain. Spinning, spinning, pussycat, pussycat, where have you been? Cats with glowing sticks, pretty lights, pretty pretty.

Everything is black. He tries to move, tries to blink his eyes. A sliver of light, then it's gone. C'mon, Jocko. Focus. You're the guy in charge.

Then he sees a grey glow, a faint glimmer on the black horizon. The dim light rolls away, then reappears, like he's tumbling through space.

Now the light rushes at him and the darkness vanishes. He's in sickbay. Right, that makes sense. Wisps of memory swirl, coalesce. There were doctors, and wounded soldiers laid out on gurneys, Gizmo and the Krang. Shit, what happened to the Krang? Where's Gizmo? Who's running this show?

Jocko forces his eyes to focus. He sees rows of empty gurneys. He looks left. looks right. The empty gurneys swing back and forth as he shifts his eyes. Wait, holy shit, he's moving his eyes. Gizmo, are you there? Gizmo? He's shouting in his head and the thought bothers him. He shakes it away, realizes his head is shaking when he tells it to. What the hell is happening?

He's raising his left hand, staring at it, when the doc appears.

"Welcome back, Sergeant Pierce."

Jocko blinks at the doc, then at his raised hand. He wills the fingers to move, and they do. Then he laughs aloud.

"You need to take it easy, Sergeant. You've been out for three days. Take it slow."

"What about the Krang?"

"They're gone. Took their new parts and vanished. Lifted off Sector Seven not long after that. But before they left, they fixed you. After you collapsed, the head Krang had a look at you.

"He found the implant system at the back of your skull. He insisted we remove it. It was your soldiers who backed him up. Graves and Gates. The captain was against it."

Jocko reaches a hand to the nape of his neck, feels the bandage.

"What about Gizmo?"

"Sorry? Who?"

"Nothing. Never mind. I'm still a little fuzzy."

But Jocko Pierce isn't fuzzy at all. Scenes flash through his brain, each one sharp and vivid. Gizmo, the idea for the coup stick, the fight with the Krang, he remembers it all, right up to the moment the lights went out. Now Gizmo is gone. And all the gurneys are empty.

"Doc, what happened to the wounded?"

"Up and around, every one of them. Well, we lost one. We thought it would be two, but we were able to save Corporal Benson. We used the implant unit we removed from you. He's waiting to see you, by the way."

"Who, Benson?"

Yes. He's been waiting for two days. The captain gave up on you, said you were dead for sure this time. But Corporal Benson didn't believe him. He's just outside, with Gates and Graves. Shall I send them in?"

"You damn skippy, Doc. By all means, send them in."

The doctor disappears. Jocko hears a shuffling of feet, then three faces smiling down at him. Gates, tough and pretty at the same time, Graves' ugly mug, and Corporal Benson. Gates does the talking, like always.

"Hey, Top. How ya feeling?"

"I feel like six gallons of shit in a five-gallon bucket, but it'll pass. You guys okay? Who's running the show?"

"Lieutenant Gregg is doing the honors. Captain sort of checked himself out, I guess. Speaking of which, me and Graves gotta head back. We're on duty but we skipped out."

"Which means you two clowns are away from your post. Get your asses back there, and I do mean now."

"Roger that, Top."

Graves and Gates turn to go, but Jocko stops them.

"Hey you two grunts. Thank you."

"Sure, Top."

And then they're gone. Corporal Benson hovers over Jocko's gurney, grinning a stupid grin. Jocko remembers that Benson was never the sharpest knife in the drawer.

"You okay, Corporal?"

"Yes, Jocko, I am right as rain as the saying goes."

Anger shoots through Jocko like an electric current. This low-life grunt has the nerve to call him Jocko? A goddamn First Sergeant? This kid is going to be on extra duty for an earth year at least.

He opens his mouth to shout, sees the smirk on Benson's face, and a weird gleam in his eye. The realization sinks in with a jolt.

"Gizmo? Holy shit! Is that you?"

"Yes, Jocko, it's me. They implanted me on Benson. The poor lad is gone, I'm afraid. Really gone."

"Shit. It's always hard losing a young one, and it never gets easier. But we've got work to do and you're on duty, Corporal Benson. Your first duty is to tell me everything I missed, starting with when I blacked out."

"You got it, Top."

Corporal Benson pulls up a stool beside First Sergeant Pierce.

When the doctor hurries into sickbay to check on his last patient, he sees young Corporal Benson and the craggy sergeant huddled together, heads close. Their conversation strikes him as intense and deeply private. The doc makes a notation on a clipboard, then backs away without saying a word.

EASY ANSWERS

Diana Olney

At fifteen
I already knew
what I wanted to be:
Perfect.
It wasn't hard.
Perfection was simple;
a basic equation
I could solve
in my sleep.

I didn't need to be good
at math,
or science, or language,

or even history
to pass the test,
not when all the answers
were right in front of me—
displayed, framed,
captured,
printed and plastered
on every cover, every poster,
every wall, every screen.

Night after night,
I dreamt
in colors
of paint-by-numbers:
Thirty-one,
twenty-three,
thirty-two
into a size zero
little black dress.

That was the magic number
I wanted to wear:
a digit so small, so slender,
there was no room for error.

But zero has plenty of space
for good things—
the kind that come
to those who wait
until there's nothing
left
to lose.

The more I lost,
the more I gained—
beauty, power,

mystery, grace;
plus a healthy dose
of envy and infatuation.
One by one,
I collected them all,
wore them like charms,
and ate them like candy.

I had to do a little math
to make it all fit,
but that was no problem,
any grade-school kid
can add and subtract—
skip a meal,
pop a pill,
flush a mistake.
Lather, rinse, repeat.
It was an easy routine.
By sixteen,
I had almost everything.

Almost
was a nice place to visit.
So close
to perfection,
I could taste it—
as long as I didn't eat.

Too bad I couldn't stay.

I thought I had all the answers.
The mirror didn't agree.
The halls of my temple
were bare,
empty,
but outside,

the frame was full
of things I never asked for—
dark things,
hungry things,
things with bones like razors,
skin like paper,
eyes like holes,
and limbs like needles;
things that had grown
while I was shrinking.

I ran from the mirror
straight to the scale.
I stood,
I waited,
I prayed
for an easy answer.
But the one I wanted
never came.
Somehow, I'd passed it by
without ever knowing
I was there.

It was too late
to go back,
according to the scale.
No matter how long
I waited,
or how much
I begged,
the numbers didn't change,
all they did
was shrink,
falling
further and further
from grace.

That's when I found out:
Perfection is easy to get,
but hard to keep.

MECHANICAL DINNER

Nathaniel Barrett

For once, Grant Thompson's shift at Innovative Robotics Incorporated did not go overtime. After a brief and convenient ride on his city's autonomous bus-line, he returned to his apartment building at exactly 5:30pm. On this evening commute, Grant wasn't distracted by the neon billboards advertising VR movies and automatic blanket-folders, nor the programmed flow of electric buses carrying residents atop a railway 100 feet above the city floor. No, all he *really* thought about was eating dinner with his family. His wife and two sons motivated Grant to persevere through the recurring tediums of the workday.

Grant just hoped they could avoid errors this time. He *really* hoped they could.

Inside the sliding doors of his apartment's lobby, the soft tangerine glow of lamps mimicked the radiance of a sunset. Heaters lining the walls and floor blanketed Grant in a crisp warmness. Blue couches which offered free massages encircled the lobby's perimeter. Grant considered getting one; he longed to sink deep into the navy fabric and rub away the aches which have lingered in his spine and shoulders from years of building robots. Nevertheless, his family expected him, and so Grant ignored the small things like bodily pains. He darted toward the elevators, not wanting to leave his two hungry sons waiting any longer.

A shrill voice stopped Grant. Jeanine, the elderly secretary who was more entertained by the lives of the residents than her own, had to speak to Grant first, of course. "Hey, how're you hanging in there?" she asked.

"Good," Grant said. "But work is hard."

"I can only imagine. Especially with all you've been through."

Grant shrugged.

"Have you been managing your losses any better?"

"Losses?" Grant's right palm fidgeted, and his eyes felt like they were being drilled. "Sorry. I don't know what you're talking about."

Jeanine sighed. She contorted her facial muscles to grin artificially at Grant. "Yeah, I'm not sure why I said that, and I'm sorry for saying it. Have a good night, Grant."

Grant beamed. "You do the same."

He turned around and walked away, not seeing Jeanine sulk and convulse through her wrinkled cheeks behind him.

At last, Grant stood in front of the steel elevators. Cameras scanned his face and verified his identity, and then the metallic doors slid open to a carpeted chamber. Grant strapped himself into a couch in the center of the elevator. Lights the color of lavender, his favorite color, filled the space as the doors closed. Although he had sat on the couch numerous nights before, it felt uniquely comfortable each time Grant collapsed onto it. It was so comfortable, in fact, that Grant didn't even *feel* the elevator moving as it brought him back to his apartment. And yet, the doors reopened to the sight of his mudroom no more than ten seconds after they closed.

Grant stepped off the elevator and was home.

Grant's wife, Margaret Thomspon, rotated from the kitchen to greet Grant. She wore the same checker apron she wore every day, and smiled the same warm smile that calmed Grant after difficult days. "Welcome home, honey. How was work?" she asked.

"Over with," Grant said. "In all seriousness, though, it was pretty decent. I don't have to work overtime today, and I've been meaning to spend more time with you and the boys."

Grant's two small sons, Johnny and Tiger, bounded into the mudroom to greet him. Johnny was the older of the two and had a face peppered with small freckles. He was too short and too slender, even for a boy his age. Tiger, meanwhile, had already developed muscle at the age of seven. His hair bent to the left side of his head, and he lost two of his front teeth from a hard tackle at football practice years ago.

"Dad. Dad," the boys said, as they dashed over and hugged Grant. "We cannot believe you are back this early."

"Settle down, guys." An icy sharpness shot up Grant's hand as he pried the boys' cold bodies from his legs. At least their hair was soft, Grant thought while he ruffled their little heads with his oil-coated palms.

"Dinner is ready, honey," Margaret chirped on cue. "I made your favorite dish, tangy chicken breast."

"You're the best, Margs!" Grant said. "Let's eat."

Margaret, Johnny, and Tiger marched into their spots in the dining room. Grant staggered in behind them. Robotic arms sprouted from the walls and placed the plates and utensils onto the table. Once everything was set, the arms opened the oven and pulled out Margaret's steamy piece of chicken. Dinner, like most household chores, could have easily been automated, but

Margaret insisted she be the one to make it. She enjoyed cooking; it was her creative outlet in a mechanized world.

The family sat down for dinner.

"So, Tiger, how was football practice?" Grant asked, leaving his chicken half eaten on his plate.

"It was good," Tiger said. "I tackled two kids and intercepted three throws."

"Hah hah, that's my boy! We don't call em' Tiger for nothing--ain't that right, Margs?"

"Yes. He surely is the athlete of the family," Margaret said.

"How about you, Johnny Boy? How'd school go? What about that math test?" Grant asked with a strained grin.

"My day was good, thank you," Johnny said. He smiled with perfect symmetry. Johnny was the more polite child, and Margaret used to call him *Little King Arthur*.

"Unfortunately, I failed that math test. I am sorry, Dad. I should have studied the multiplication table more."

Grant sighed, trying to convey a sense of disappointment to Johnny. "I thought we went over this, son. Didn't you tell me that you were going to spend 20 minutes studying for it each day?"

"We did."

"Yes, we did," Grant said. "Starting tonight, I expect you to study every day. Cause' if there is a next time, then let's just say you'd have your TV privileges revoked, capisce?"

"Yes, Dad. I will do better next time," Johnny said, his face unflushed and his smile still plastered on his face.

"You're a smart kid, Johnny, and no math test is ever gonna make me stop loving you. You've just gotta apply yourself more, bud."

"Thanks, Dad."

Grant took a few minutes to eat the rest of his chicken. Nobody spoke in these moments, so nothing was heard, save for the grandfather clock, whose ticking stalked Grant's ears.

Then Grant's phone rang. He apologized to his family and removed himself from the table. Grant stepped into the living room and inspected the call. It was from a number he didn't recognize. Grant stared at the screen for a moment, ambivalent as to whether or not he should accept the call. He decided to take it; maybe it was from a co-worker he hadn't saved in his phone yet?

Grant lifted the device up to his ear and a voice passed through it. *Grant, we need to-*

Grant hung up and turned off his phone. It was his Mother, again. A few months ago, he had programmed his phone to automatically reject calls from both his parents and in-laws, so they must've gotten a new phone number. Grant wasn't going to speak with them, not at least until he finished what he needed to complete. Hopefully, they'd understand him a little better when they see the final product.

Grant lurched into the dining room and clapped his hands. The robotic arms reemerged from the walls to sweep the kitchen and wash the dishes. Only Grant's family remained at the table, sitting on steel chairs and staring into space.

"We should watch a movie together," Grant announced.

"We would love to, honey. What movie would you like to see?" Margaret asked, her head shifting to stare at Grant.

"How bout' the new Barry Dunning movie? I heard it's got good reviews," Grant said.

"Yes," said Tiger, as if he was addressing the air, "let us go watch that movie."

As Grant walked to the living room his family echoed his movements, trailing like shadows behind him. When they arrived in their living room, Grant and Margaret huddled together on a leather couch, and Tiger and Johnny sat on two little green chairs.

The television was positioned below a crystal blue window, and, because their apartment was on the top floor, their view perched between the city's tallest lights and the lowest radiance of the stars. Some nights after dinners long ago, Grant and his family would watch the stars roll above the Earth. Grant and Margaret taught many things about the universe to the boys during those days. But deep down, Grant used to be indifferent to the stars. The only universe he needed gravitated on his side of the window. Yet after *it* happened, the family did not bother to look up at space anymore. As of late, Grant spent a whole lot more time thinking about that other side of the window.

Grant turned on the TV. The movie played immediately; he had already set this particular one up two nights ago. It began on a highway, where a man was driving a car with his wife and daughters. The family talked and talked: about their days, about their relatives, about their lives. Then the truck came from straight ahead of them. It was a blur at first, deep within the corner of their eyes. But it emerged quickly--breaching their pupils and paralyzing their minds. The children in the back screamed, not old enough to know what was about to happen, but animal enough to sense the strength of the charging vehicle. The man swerved right. And as the car flew into the air, the woman next to him was silent, everything happening too fast for her to have any final thoughts at all.

The television flicked off; the empty static mocked Grant. He bent into his lap and sobbed. Margaret, Tiger, and Johnny stared at Grant, as if awaiting for some sort of instruction. But nothing came of it, for Grant's empathy program had failed again, so his family was still incapable of being sad.

Deep into the night, Grant continued to cry. He stopped sometime around 3 am, when Tiger, Johnny, and Margaret powered down from a lack of use.

Grant was going to have to work overtime, after all. His family was far from complete enough to replicate who they were before the accident two years ago. Even if Grant somewhat expected it, the failure of their wiry minds still overloaded his blood-filled heart.

Fortunately, Grant had the weekend ahead of him to work on their programs. If robots were to replace his dead family, they must be capable of sadness.

TO THE MEGALITHS OF MONSTROSITY AND BEYOND

D.G. Ironside

"There is a mouse," Jadus said, eyes down, "that guards the boundaries of what is known."

I chugged another tankard of well-crafted ale, one of the creations from the brewmasters at *Overhaul House*. Jadus and I loved to explore pubs that were dedicated to personal improvement.

"A mouse!" I guffawed, working up a burp to relieve my distension, the stiff roundness of my belly. I did so, belching out the first seven letters of the alphabet. Then I brashly relieved a niggling itch upon my nuggets.

"Yes, indeed," murmured Jadus, as if my boorish display had sparked his memory. My man was concentrating, holding his forehead over bent elbow, mulling a puzzle that combined clues and intersected words, the latest thing to hit Bardelve's most whimsical periodical, which was to say, the flaming gossip of the *Recurrent Rubdown*, printed on wax tablets.

"What's a twelve-letter word for 'totally lacking in truth'?" Jadus asked me, still engrossed.

"What-Jadus-say," I replied, rather glibly. "A mouse at the edge of the world, indeed."

"I thought we were past that, but yes, a mouse," Jadus said, even more ponderous and distracted. "There is one hint I've just read here about cute little critters. It wafted past my memory, a derelict tale of children's lore." I stared at the top of Jadus' head and saw luscious brown skin under the blackest hair, my sweet man, my lover, strange guardian of wayward fables. Before I could drunkenly contemplate the figurative ramifications of such bizarre allegory, a rodent's role inside a myth, Gregor the Ineffable strode into the place, our boss, the driver of the slaves, us.

He looked larger, darker, hairier, and much more sweaty than usual in unseasonal all-black garb. His thigh-high boots smacked the floorboards, much too much for summer. As we knew, his evil visage and broad black beard were only a harsh veneer that facilitated the more heinous of his deeds. In truth, he was only forty-nine percent villain, the rest of him a mess of bubbling impertinence, low-throttled rage, and inchoate desires. All his hugeness came within range, swollen muscle, and foul fume.

"I thought you diddleweeds were supposed to leave yesterday," Gregor spat.

Jadus didn't even look up.

"My lovely man here is rather submerged in his word puzzle. For myself, I am plodding inexorably towards the full measure of intoxication." I gave myself another good scratch. "But be assured that we are moving out in the morning."

"Kalvus, you are certainly consistent," Gregor said. "As it happens, it's lucky I caught you. I have one more tidbit on the Megaliths of Monstrosity."

Those stone monuments were our new objective, the lingering construct of a long-dead and near-forgotten empire. The ring of rocks was also the rumoured burial site of Carmino Eleganto, great warrior-prince of antiquity and wanderer of every fanciful realm. According to the foggy inventions of legend, Carmine bore a magical chariot that flew, a blue diamond spear of sorcerous power, and a remarkable bronze whistle that summoned a thousand-thousand canaries, together to pull his vehicle cross the skies. None of that seemed to Jadus and me more than whimsical hyperbole, but Gregor the Insatiable always wanted astonishing stuff. He was utterly obsessed with so many fantastic, amazing things, and it was forever up to us to go and fetch.

"I was playing cards the other night at the *Ribald Room* and Fandango the wizard was there, attempting to make good on his tab," Gregor explained.

"Fandango's not much of a wizard," Jadus said, finally turning his eyes up, only to illustrate his contempt.

Gregor huffed and countered, "He's not a wizard at all. 'Wizard' isn't even a real thing. You know just as well as I." He made those quote marks with his hands. "But Fandango does know a bit about ill-conceived magic as it relates to gambling. Since he'd wagered his naval on the dice, I'd figured I'd finger in there for a piece of the action."

I pondered this. I thought to ask. I let it go.

"Since the dice came up as a hard eight, he lost, and I won, four on the floor and holes bored for more," our boss said, holding his arms and elbows.

"And?" I asked.

"Either I got to bugger his bellybutton, or the equivalent in compensation," Gregor explained. "He forked out many secrets."

"What's an eight-letter word for nonsense and exaggeration?" I offered. Whenever I was drunk, I assumed myself to be quite clever.

"Exactly," said Gregor. "But from all he spewed, I got something useful. Late last year, Fandango funded his own expedition, sending a trio of raiders to the Megaliths. Two of them never returned. Like us, they were seeking the remains of Prince Carmine. The one dude who made it back claimed his two buddies disappeared into nothing."

"A portal?" I asked.

"Another dimension?" Jadus conjectured, palm returning to chin.

"Something," Gregor the Speculative agreed. "Just make sure you don't do the same. I want that whistle."

I giggled, rather infused with bewilderment. I asked, "Of the three grand things we're after, you desire to summon a thousand-thousand birds?".

"Yeah. I want to impress a girl," Gregor said.

"If we summon a thousand-thousand canaries, just for some woman, you're going to need an awful lot of seed," Jadus supposed.

"That's the idea," said Gregor.

We had crossed an immense and sweeping plain of grass to seek the Monstrous Megaliths. A notable thing about a formation of immense standing rocks, we understood, was the dearth of hills. My horse appreciated the sure footing and the lack of incline, but my eyes regretted the vacant look. As far as the end, there was only beige, yellow and green, swaying in the summer breeze. It seemed all the grass listened to a powerful ballad, waving altogether with the stink of rot offset by wildflowers.

Later, as the air came more still, the landscape became swept with drifting pollen, which irritated my nose and was aiming to make my horse choke, so thick it was. There were masses of fluff appearing as miniature clouds, floating goldenrod, ready to induce a sneezing fit and entice the rubbing of itchy eyes unto madness.

Jadus had not the sensitivity I did, and he only chortled to see me hack and snort, the trickle of snot running over my lips. My chin was sopped with the outpouring of goo. I halted my mount and stepped down into a field that was lush, long blades and spikelets reaching my chest. The plants were so thickset that a lion could have sprung out unseen and unheard. For my suffering nose I could have been eaten alive and called it relief.

"Here. Overdose on limes," Jadus told me. He bent down to hand me a clutch of green citrus, four in one hand. "Something in these works against sneezing," he said. "Go ahead. I packed us the gimlet limes that grow at Zaris' Cathedral of Compassion."

Brilliant. I began to tear the limes apart, desperate for a panacea. The goddess Zaris was a mischievous seraph of mercy, and her fruits would be infused with blessings, likely mixed, but I could not care. The juice of any old lime could blind and sting, but these fruits were ambrosia to my swollenness. I ate them and smeared the peelings over all of my head. The space behind my nose drained out in a whoosh.

"Now you smell like polished furniture," Jadus joked.

"Or late-summer pie with cream for the top," I agreed.

"Um, your cream is suddenly not on the top," my boyfriend said with a grin.

I felt my face. Oh, Zaris! The limes had cured me but transformed me. It had happened all at once. My hair was lengthened to curl past my shoulders, my skin softened to velour, my boots two sizes too big. I was not of my maleness at all as my waist pulled in and my chest pushed out. In moments, I could identify myself no longer. I hesitated to reach about and down, to ascertain whatever was for certain. For sure, my clothes were loose, and perhaps I was as well. I would absolutely need new shoes, in any case, several pairs.

Before I could think any further, the grasses moved, the sign showing more than just wind. A gnarl was heard, movement, something fast. I twisted my head, trying to catch up with the flashing and dashing.

"Climb your horse!" Jadus ordered, thinking to save our mounts. As I put my foot in the stirrup, something spoke.

"Terrible twosome is here," it whispered, a sweet and sinister voice.

"You've obviously played backgammon with us before," I said, sounding eerily like my older sister. I had an immediate urge to find a bathroom and hog it all to myself. Instead, I removed my dainty grip off the horn and cantle and let my foot down. I looked about, having no good guess at location.

"Speak again, sprite of the grass," Jadus said, tilting his neck from his saddle.

I reached for my dagger, for all that I would likely poke out my eye or impale my newly delicate hand.

"Don't," said Jadus.

"I'm the one down here, loverman," I said, again with a foreign and gentle lilt. I shook my head in disbelief of myself, only to see traced lines atop the grass, making so many fronds sway. I tingled. We were not alone. Death always comes as a secret, strong enough for a modified man.

"No. No. No!" the voice hissed. It was close, the sound of something diminutive. I imagined an imp, some devilish spirit that would dance on my shoulder before biting off my bottom lip. Instead, it appeared near my boot on the trampled grass, a chubby thing with a squarish head and huge pointed ears. It was green and yellow and furry, like a short and rotund otter-monkey without a tail. My horse was spooked when the fat little fairy thing tickled its leg. The mount bucked and nearly kicked me in the chin before it ran off, a near miss that would have knocked me to oblivion. Wavered, I hit the ground with a thud, only to see Jadus run off, chasing my horse with his own. It was difficult to observe my shallow place on the priority list in real time.

I was face to face with the plump fey creature, less than two feet tall. At my range, I could see its weird and wonderful jade fur, bulbs of clarion yellow for eyes. I clamoured to lean on my hands, working to inhale a breath. On the ground, the area smelled of wet dirt, dying plants, and the work of worms.

"You's bad lady, come here," it said in a hiss. It appeared quite disturbed for something so cute, shielding its gaze with one hand and peeking. My newfound femininity was on shameless display through the plunge of my shirt. I grabbed my ample double front and held it together. As I tempered my modesty, I endured what was an odd moment of isolation and intimacy.

"Just who or what are you?" I asked of the thing, the little pudgy green humanoid-hominid. It was more than that, I could tell, from its faint scent of mint and an odd tingling aura.

"I is Hoobah, buckawn, spring leaf, grass land sentry," it spoke. When I went to get to my knees, it pulled forth a tiny blade, a miniature point conjured as if from the air, and by the sharpness of it, bid me stay down. Nothing like being ordered about by the manifestation of a fable. I imagined I was a delinquent child about to be abducted or worse, some gruesome lesson to come. I swallowed a lump of warm embarrassment, sweat drizzling down my stupid head, the back of my neck, my dangling hair all about. For my hands holding my shirt, I couldn't do a thing with it.

"Oh, grass lord Hoobah," I said carefully, "you have cleverly startled my horse and left me at your mercy. What might I do for you here, to convey respect to you?"

"You's shut yer tongue trap and says no more,'" it bade me with a scowl. I did. As I paused, I listened, trying to detect Jadus and the horses. There was nothing but the wind. I was alone and trapped with this little beast. I had been captured by a children's toy, of the fluffy variety.

"You's come to endless plains," Hoobah said with his brows furrowed, offhand shielding his face. It was as if he was trying to be commanding but deftly avoiding the fullness of my gaze.

"Fer's why?" Hoobah asked.

I considered lying, my default position. Instead, as an impulsive novelty, I experimented boldly with the truth.

"My man and I are headed to the Megaliths of Monstrosity," I offered.

"Bah! Stupid name!" the buckawn spat.

"Uh, okay then," I countered. "As it happens, I did not originate the name. I only repeat the moniker mentioned to me."

"Rocks bigga bigga!" he said.

"I would argue that 'rocks bigga bigga' is also a rather silly and unfortunate name. Is that the official title of the boulders, or your own descriptor?"

"No! Dum-dum lady," it said. "You's think rocks smaller than they is." Again, he only peeked to see me. When he did glance, his look changed each time. I did not very much understand, but assumed I was distinctly repulsive as a female of the species.

I shook my head and tried to focus. I wondered how far we were from the Megaliths. If this plump buckawn was a local denizen of these environs, he might know critical truths. He could possess the very keys to the burial place of Carmino Eleganto, in addition to knowing its precise location. Or I could merely be dealing with a stuffed plaything with a piss-poor attitude.

"Truly, my wee master," I said, "we label the rocks Monstrous and believe them to be so. Might you tell me the last time you walked between them?"

He grunted. He looked again, once more not in total control of his faculties. He blinked, he sighed, his obstructed vision constraining his emotion. I realized then, quite suddenly, that I had it all backward. I was not disgusting at all, but strangely and strongly alluring, an entirely new feeling for me. Remarkably, I had been transformed into a gorgeous creature and Hoobah was trying mightily to be unaffected by my static comely charm. Believing this, I shifted strategy at once.

"Might you assist us, oh strong and vigilant Hoobah, with your great wisdom?" I asked, smiling sweet and as full as a mischievous feline on the branch of a tree. My new voice had a sultriness, a sand, a silk, and sure enough, Hoobah could not ignore it.

"You means tempt me, fool me," Hoobah said sheepishly, trying and failing to brandish his small thin javelin. It appeared as a long needle for leather, strangely shiny, its razor point glinting.

"Not I, no. I would never. I only want to see those rocks with my own little eyes," I said melodically. I held up one hand in a placating gesture of delicious fingers. Absently, I traced a line on my collar bone with one finger and wondered what the hell had come over me.

"Dem rocks gonna make you go gone! Gets you what you deserve!" He was suddenly quite enraged. This little lord of the fescue had a grudge against people, even if something of Zaris' clever magic was captivating him. He rubbed his own cheeks, doing everything he could to keep his eyes away. For myself, I played delicately with the ringlets in my tresses.

"Stop dat!" he demanded.

I contemplated the stupid thing I was trying to do. Whatever it was, I believed I was struggling to make it look natural. Then again, I was brand spanking new at whatever gals do.

"But great and glorious Hoobah, I only mean—"

Somehow, he resisted me and gathered himself.

"You's the weirdest! Stoopid stoopid!" With that, he lunged forward, fast like a snake, and he stabbed me in the cheek, an inch below my right eye. His weapon plunged, hit bone, and bounced.

I howled and fell backward, reeling, clutching at my face for having been seriously stung. There were tiny footsteps as Hoobah ran and wove himself into the grass, giving forth fading cackles as I thrashed. I felt foul heat enter my blood. I peered through the clutch of my digits to view flattened grass alone, and

I detected an emptiness to know that Hoobah was gone. Jadus trotted to appear right then, on his horse with mine in tow.

"You alright?" he asked.

"No," I replied, feeling my lips grow fat, every bit of me having fire beneath the skin. Something malignant was in my veins and working to shutter my throat. My heart pounded hard like I was naked and ready, for an end much less pleasurable than usual. Despite my desperation, I instantly could not help but ponder that climax, torn between the acid in my face and the novel crack of possibility. Between pangs of pain, I thought of tulips for the briefest iota. Then I wept with unbeckoned emotion.

"The furry little bastard stabbed me!" I wailed to Jadus, holding my wounded cheek. My words were thick, my tongue expanding to dangerous proportion.

"You're blowing up like a gas bladder," Jadus said, eyes wide. He made quick to dismount.

"There's irony," I uttered, trying, and failing to stand. "Because this time, I set loose the truth instead of inflating lies."

"You've never been very good at veracity," I heard Jadus say. I saw my man turn to a blur as my eyes began to shut. I was plunging into thick blackness, where I expected no more chances, no more buttery dreams.

"My time as a woman appears to be at an end," I uttered, as he to moved me, cradling my head upon his lap.

"That's okay," he said in a hushed tone. "I never cared much for innies, anyway."

That was the last I heard, before my mind fell down a hole.

By the sweetest angels of deception, I lived. In the fog of my terrible vision, I swore to never tell a true story again.

"Keep yourself still," Jadus told me. He was only a grey form, blotting the sun. I was on my back on a hard surface, a stoney patch of ground by the feel on my hands. I was in waking coma of dull aching, all senses poorly arrayed.

"Where..." I began.

"Shhh."

Jadus then explained to me details of what I'd missed. I only stayed recumbent and performed a self inventory. I felt my eyes on the verge of collapse, my nose useless, my body destroyed, my mouth full of goo. It was a vivid flashback to my tawdry youth, all the sad consequences of sensory abuse and none of the pleasant precursors. I appeared dressed just as then, which was to say, hardly at all.

Before I could ask a single question, a hum, a thrum, a vibration came to my notice and amplified in strength. Jadus stopped where he was and gasped. The air thickened with the sound, becoming so rich that I swore it was turning to liquid. I coughed, ready to drown. I froze, as if time was nothing. I could hear Jadus speak to me, but his voice was lost in the viscous atmosphere, nothing more than bubbles in a freaky transparent ocean. I believed I could see his words, his sounds, as floating effervescence suspended in gel, the bizarre space between us.

With a strange swiftness the grass around us grew, from a low landscape of which I was not aware, to huge mounds of it all about, tall tufts, long blades vacillating, submerged for moment in an all-flowing atmospheric river. Then, just as soon as the transformation began, it ended. The humming faded. We were once again in breathable air. I made a rough sound to expunge the mucus from my centre. With monumental effort and an old dame's command, I made to stand. Internal air escaped me from the zenith and the nadir in a shameful show.

"Dammit all, Jadus," I cursed. "You didn't tell me I'd become more decrepit than dust."

"Be careful," he said, grabbing me, his nose ready for it. "Your body is still recovering from the buckawn's poison and Zaris' magic."

"Ugh," he continued with a shallow breath. "That's some wet dust."

I teetered and looked about. We were standing in the shadows of the Monstrous Megaliths, huge wide rectangles of epic bleakness that made me shiver. They were a circle of upright stones that towered the sky, nine rough obelisks of beige and cream, the extracted foundations of a mountain. Larger than anything possible, they hummed, I swore, low and ominous, threatening at a second to make the grass and air change again. On each flat boulder was a mass of symbols and runes, carved in deepest black, and each figure stamped in stone would have been bigger than my entire body. I felt small, smaller than usual, shrivelled as from a mid-winter bath in a lake of ice. Or so I thought. I remembered and at last reached for my box of gears. Instead, I found a hot potato salad.

"Have the limes shown no signs of wearing off?" I asked.

"I had to apply more limes to relieve the effects of Hoobah's mini-blade," Jadus told me. I sighed.

"The sorcery of changing is even more profound," he said, looking at me quite strange. He peeled his gawk away. "I'm sure it isn't permanent," he offered. "Forget all that. Focus instead on what's before us."

I looked out and upward at a mystery beyond my weak yet lithe body. I was dumbfounded. All these years I had been aware of these massive stones in the distant reaches of my memory, a construct the rough remnant of an ancient culture that worshipped the sun and stars. Many an inebriated tale had described mystic natural power and fertility rituals with nubile youth fitting all their delicate parts together. My thoughts abruptly imagined those details as I never could before. That penetrating mystery aside, I felt no humans could have constructed such an unfathomable cluster of standing stones.

"From a distance, the menhirs appeared no higher than three men, standing on each other's shoulders..." Jadus said.

"Just how do those three balanced men keep themselves erect?" I asked, fingering a tall stalk of grass.

"Mind yourself, Kalvus."

I looked above us, a big empty blue, not one cloud. The vault of the sky carried on, out to multitudinous horizons at every degree, for what we could observe for the sea of grass. Not one tree, not one bird. I listened, looked, and sniffed. I felt the air. There was not a single insect to intrude upon the landscape. No more buzz than a tavern of temperance.

"We are not at home," I claimed, absent of breath. Jadus caught me from my near swoon. His hands felt odd, rough, different, strong. Right at that second, I had a warm inkling.

"You sure you aren't curious?" I asked, squeezing at him from within his muscled grasp. We were alone in the great outdoors, but his was a snoozing snake.

"Mind your hands and keep yourself to the task at hand, girlfriend."

"Aren't I your darling? Don't you love me anymore?" I asked, coy, my perfect chin upon my white shoulder. Jadus only lifted me to vertical and set me straight.

"Uh, yeah, you are, and I do. But you know what I like, Kalvus. It would be like trying to pick a lock with a small bit of rope. Those finer strokes, you can try yourself when you have a moment alone. We have work to do. Now get dressed." I huffed and did. I stuffed my loose boots with grass for a snugger fit, no improvement for the janky look.

Jadus gathered up our few things. We found the horses amid the tallness of the stalks. Climbing on their backs, we saw more details of the surround. Amid the Megaliths were supernatural shadows, a black-grey shroud with eerie tendrils of electric flow, a conjuring of pure power or the colloquial aesthetic of another world. At that point, I knew I concurred with Jadus' notions. He had told me that somehow, we had crossed over the unseen threshold of which Gregor the Augur had warned us. The Megaliths appeared twenty feet tall from some finite range and now, two hundred at least. We were inside some pocket plane, a strange facet of reality, and I had missed the moment of transition.

"Let us dare go to the clearing," he said, pointing. There was an area of low grass within the circle of Megaliths where walking would be possible, and answers might be closer. Yet the horses were spooked as if ghosts were in their ears, near impossible to control, and when we reached the ring of the grand stones, we were forced to dismount. Even Jadus' sweet touch could not ease them, and they bolted.

"We're on our own now," I said, warily.

"I didn't believe we'd be riding home, anyhow," Jadus agreed, somber.

We stepped forward, becoming aware of a flat circle of stone at the centre of the Megaliths, a measure of rock embedded and flush with the earth. We approached and were shocked when giant Hoobah emerged from behind the largest of the upright stones.

"Uzza-babah!" he said, his voice like thunder. His huge feet fell from his jump, shaking the ground for his great weight.

He was the same in proportion as I saw him before, but now twenty feet tall, his little razor point grown to an enormous sliver of radiant blue. It was clear. It was the diamond spear of Carmino Eleganto he bore. Jadus and I struggled to catch our breath. We held up our hands like petty criminals, quick to surrender.

"Oh, mighty Hoobah," I said, dropping to my knees.

Jadus remembered the description from my previous encounter and submitted just the same. The hulking buckawn growled, his shape twisting with fierce muscle under his gold-green fur. Now he was a champion of nature, beyond question, a huge and fierce guardian. A stuffy doll he still was, but enormous, ready to stab, and to crush if the need arose.

"Somebody got the ball in the milk jug," Jadus whispered. "Don't let me die at the hand of some toy from a carnival." I reached and clutched his hand, my own digits at half strength and so soft I could swear I'd soaked them in lotion. My velvet touch only gave Jadus the willies. He shuddered and as he did, I plotted to attempt my seductive moves again.

"Oh, Hoobah," I called. He looked at me with his big yellow eyes and postured with the flow of rage.

"You's come to rocks bigga bigga!" he shouted, all sinew and fury, occupying the entire diameter of the flat round stone beneath.

"We have," I said. "I survived your little stab to the head, when we were still in the world that I call home. I am quite lucky."

"I exist many places!" the greater version of Hoobah howled. The sky seemed to echo him with thunderous discontent. He was a wee thing in my home plane, but a giant for the moment, commanding the very essence of the land, the Megaliths, the grassland.

"I's try to keep you away!" Hoobah exclaimed. "I's try to keep you back. People's like you never listen."

He was certainly correct on that account. Nature never gave a warning that humans did not ignore.

"Don't you's look at me! You's deal with da mouse!" Hoobah said, pointing to the ground, the broad stone circle upon which he stood. The tip of the bright spear lingered with its point over something we could not see.

"What in the world," I muttered, still on my knees.

"Oh my," Jadus breathed. His eyes seemed to see something move. We waited for just a beat.

Then, a tiny mouse appeared at the edge of the stone and stared up at us with knowing eyes. He was gray with black eyes, a little tail, impossibly cute and banal in every way. Except—

"Hello there," said the mouse.

Jadus gave a little giggle. I tittered as well, to half recollect I'd been told when I was fully in the wind, two and three-quarters sheets.

"Shut up and show's da respect!" demanded Hoobah, with a ferocious shake.

"Excuse me," the mouse said, standing on its rear legs. "If we could, I might trouble you both to take a moment to converse with me." Its voice was tiny, perfect, and polite, much like an erudite scribe or scholar.

To hear the wee rodent talk, we both settled, more reverential in our posture, whereupon Hoobah let down his weapon and stood back, leaving us in audience.

"My apologies, Mister mouse. We have come here accidently, in some manner of speaking. We mean no disrespect," offered Jadus.

"Never you mind," said the mouse, "and you need only call me 'mouse'. Many men do come here, this wondrous place between places. Most to adventure, some to innocently pass through. I must say though, we've never yet had a married couple."

I laughed uproariously at that, jiggling my new twin frontage with bold shakes. Even Jadus could not help himself and laughed along. Then we both calmed and apologized to the mouse for our incongruous mirth.

"I am so sorry for my assumption," Mouse asserted, smoothing his composure.

"Not at all," said Jadus, his chuckles fading. "We are both still single, I'm afraid."

The mouse gave an ahem and returned to the full measure of its dignity.

"Nonetheless, you have arrived here, and it is my task to govern this place, and make sure all remains well and intact. You mean to travel to some far along destination?" With this, the mouse pulled forth a beautiful and miniscule notebook, no bigger than the nail on my little finger, and the tiniest marker of charcoal, the size of a three-day whisker on my cheek, when I did possess such. From nowhere at all he conjured the cutest pair of spectacles and placed them down on his little snout.

"From here, you may go absolutely anywhere. In place, or even in time," Mouse added.

As for exactly what to say, lying smoothly and succinctly was probably the thing to do, but Jadus jumped in and caught me off guard with legitimacy.

"We seek the tomb of Carmino Eleganto, warrior-prince of antiquity."

"Ah," said Mouse, "I understand."

"You do?" Jadus asked.

I was surprised and pleased altogether, just to be following along. I was tingling for whatever might happen next.

"Of course, I do," replied Mouse, scrawling notes with a casual paw. "Many men, bandits, or looters have come for the same, all disappointed. You see, this is indeed Mister Eleganto's resting place, yes, but he entrusted all the knowledge, wealth, and artifacts of his dying society to allow for the continuance and guardianship of this stone circle, these grand monuments around you."

Jadus asked the mouse to elaborate. As the little vermin patiently did so, Hoobah eyed us suspiciously, as if gnawing on grit.

"As such," Mouse explained, "when you crossed the remnant of the cursus, and entered the territory proper of the henge, you did cross over, transcending the bounds of your temporal world to enter the mystical environs of the long barrow devoted to our Carmine. Foremost, it is his resting place for eternity, and importantly, the nexus between so many realities. But since you have come here not as wanderers and instead as would-be pillagers of the past, we cannot help you."

"No?" Jadus asked.

"No, I am afraid. Over the centuries, many want-to-be thieves have come. All such uncivil wants have been refuted. All rude ambitions swiftly quashed. You will be no exception. We shall have you dispatched forthwith."

"Dispatched?" Jadus asked with a gulp.

"Forthwith!" exclaimed Mouse.

The mouse then snapped his book shut with a measure of finality. This meant disaster if not expiration, I sensed, from the mouse's tone and noble angle of its jaw. From whatever one reads of the countenance of mice.

"But surely we have done no wrong in merely seeking out the grave, the tomb?" Jadus asked, trying to make sense of just how we had offended.

"You have to understand," said Mouse, "that I grow so weary of explaining these things time and again."

"Our apologies, oh refined and ravishing mouse at the union of the worlds," I finally chimed in. With much feminine grace, I thought. The strange sweetness of my worlds surprised myself and the mouse together. I saw the small thing flinch like it had been hit by a miniature hammer, but to it, an unquestionable blow. It reeled, deeply shook, and from that I was much inspired. I then flickered the lids of my eyes, quite evincive and purposeful, to finally see if what the writers claimed in fairy tales held a single drop.

The mouse cleared its throat. It wiggled, distinctly uncomfortable. I could not believe such nonsense had an effect, but instantly it did.

"Quit that immediately," said Mouse.

"What's that?" I asked, quite coy. I ran my tongue across my lips, not fully wanton but of course, not entirely pure. I sensed I was doing a much better job than my previous attempts with Jadus and Hoobah. Then again, neither of them was a talking small animal, the perfect target.

"You know damn well what I mean," Mouse said.

"Whatever would that be?" I cooed. I might have seduced a swordless man with my sugary fluttering. Next, I carefully chose the delicate angles of my form. The artifice felt foreign, but one must utilize the tools one has in the box.

"You cannot enthrall me just because you are a girl," Mouse said, angry, trying to sneer yet trembling all the same. "You are no princess, no virgin, no untouched lass of lore."

I was no princess; the mouse spoke true.

"Oh, but am I not? Am I not innocent, Mister mouse?" I asked, mawkish and syrupy, the lilt of my voice like the petal of a flower floating on the upturn of the air. Certainly, I had never been besmirched, my crockpot barren of a pickle or a tickle, only for the lack of time, but still.

The mouse only quivered, quite shaken, adjusting his spectacles repeatedly, and appearing to perspire, if a mouse can do such. My ridiculous attempt was working. Hoobah saw his rodent master struggling and stepped forward, wielding the diamond spear to stab flesh through. The mouse only grabbed at his own chin and raised a teeny paw. It called out.

"No! I am fine. Hoobah, stay there. I am... just fine."

Hoobah stopped where he was, a ripple of fury in the grand muscles under his fur. He growled low. The mouse looked back to me with wary eyes. I only played carelessly with the sweep of my locks, curious as they were, and adjusted the idle measure of my sultry yet virtuous look. To exert radiating beauty was intoxicating, evidently not just to my mind, but to the tilting emotions of the mouse.

"This lass, this lady," Mouse struggled, "this fine young woman... means only to ask us a small favour."

The mouse paused and bit its tongue. Hoobah then saw me too, with all of himself. I widened my eyes as big and as open as they could go, and Hoobah's whole face went soft and empathetic. I was doing nothing but win.

"A favour only, I wish, Mister mouse. As I am lonely and all alone in this fierce world, needing only the help of you sweet brave souls to make my way unfettered. Help me and I will go off to fulfill my innocent destiny."

"A bit much, don't you think?" Jadus whispered.

"What's a five-letter word for a sly bit of business?" I whispered back.

The mouse shook, as if I wielded an irresistible allure. Hoobah, as well, was moved by my helplessness, touched from my gentle sway. I thought for a moment they might each craft me a dress or string me a necklace of pearls, merely at the asking.

"Well, then, young lady," Mouse suggested, "tell us what you need, and we shall get you to the temple on time."

Overhaul House provided Jadus and I the finest masseuses in all the land, one of each of the three varieties. I watched my lover enjoying the therapeutic and the spiritual at once, four strong hands erasing every stress. The scent of lemongrass and cherub oil suffused the room, twin odors of gratification.

Through the skylight, I saw Gregor, deftly hanging on for dear life, a thousand-thousand canaries yanking him ferociously across an otherwise blank blue sky. We did hear his fretful cries and could only smile. It was a fitting end to see our boss so satisfied.

For myself, I hadn't lasted long as a lady. From the strange and quick transport home, there were two days in Bardelve where I had barely left my room. Then, finally, came seventeen massages of the third and happiest style. I knew the magic of a lime, but not a cucumber until then. Within that stretch, it happened so sudden. My hair shrunk, my full frontage disappeared, and my outie was back with a violent pop that startled the man with the rough grip on my body. That was number sixteen, with one more on my own, just to regrip the past.

"Do you think Gregor will finally be happy?" Jadus asked, face downward. He was making sure not to groan, which would always freak a masseuse out, even though they know exactly what they are doing.

"I'm not sure," I breathed. "At least he finally has the chance to soar."

"So did you," Jadus joked.

"That's not quite what I did, Jadus," I said. "But it's certainly what I am."

CONTRIBUTORS

Colton Scott Saylor is a writer and literary scholar. His non-fiction work on race and horror has been published in journals such as *Multi-Ethnic Literature of the United States* and *Journal for the Study of Radicalism*. He lives with his wife in San Jose, CA, where he teaches literature at San Jose State University.

Colombian-born, **Jhon Sánchez** arrived in NYC seeking political asylum, where he is now a lawyer. His most recent literary publications are "Handy," (Teleport Magazine and Baseline Feed Podcast), "The Chocolate Doll Cake,"(*Landing Zone Magazine*), and "On WriNting" (the other side of hope), and "United Tombs of America," (*Midway Journal*). He was awarded the Horned Dorset Colony for 2018 and the Byrdcliffe Artist Residence Program for 2019. In 2024, New Lit Salon Press will publish his collection of short stories, Enjoy a Pleasurable Death and Other Stories that Will Kill You. For updates, please visit the Facebook page @WriterJhon, Instagram jhon_author,Twitter@jhon_author. https://muckrack.com/jhon-sanchez/articles.

Cassandra O'Sullivan Sachar is a writer and associate English professor in Pennsylvania. Her horror writing has appeared in publications including *Ink Stains: A Dark Fiction Literary Anthology, The Horror Zine, The Stygian Lepus, Wyldblood Magazine,* and *Tales from the Moonlit Path.* She holds a Doctorate of Education with a Literacy Specialization from the University of Delaware and is working toward an MFA in Creative Writing at Wilkes University. She is the current fiction editor at *River and South Review.* Read her work at https://cassandraosullivansachar.com/.

Will Lennon is a writer and researcher based in Washington D.C. While freelancing for *The Daily Beast*, he filed some of the first breaking stories on the January 6 attack from the lawn of the U.S. Capitol. He holds a bachelor's degree in journalism from George Washington University, and is currently pursuing a Master's in Public Policy focused on International Security and Economic Policy. He is also an avid reader and writer of sci-fi, fantasy, horror and magical realism. His latest novelette, entitled *Skip Tracer,* is slated for publication in November.

Wayne Kyle Spitzer is an American writer, illustrator, and filmmaker. He is the author of countless books, stories and other works, including a film (*Shadows in the Garden*), a screenplay (*Algernon Blackwood's The Willows*), and a memoir (*X-Ray Rider*). His work has appeared in *MetaStellar—Speculative fiction and beyond, subTerrain Magazine: Strong Words for a Polite Nation* and *Columbia: The Magazine of Northwest History,* among others. He holds a Master of Fine Arts degree from Eastern Washington University, a B.A. from Gonzaga University, and an A.A.S. from Spokane Falls Community College. His recent fiction includes *The Man/Woman War* cycle of stories as well as the *Dinosaur Apocalypse Saga*. He lives with his sweetheart Ngoc Trinh Ho in the Spokane Valley.

Eleanor Mourante spends her time creating mythology and writing about faraway places. She's currently working on a series of interconnected novels and novellas about psychopomps and those fighting to save the living from the creatures of the hereafter. She's ND and disabled and can occasionally be found on twitter @eatthesouls.

Marco Etheridge is a writer of prose, an occasional playwright, and a part-time poet. He lives and writes in Vienna, Austria. His work has been featured in more than eighty reviews and journals across Canada, Australia, the UK, and the USA. *U6 Stories:*

Vienna Underground Tales is Marco's latest collection of short fiction. When he isn't crafting stories, Marco is a contributing editor and layout grunt for a new 'Zine called Hotch Potch. Author website: https://www.marcoetheridgefiction.com/

Diana Olney is a Seattle based fiction author, and words are her world. Her stories have appeared in several independent publications, and her debut novella was released last year in a collaborative book. She is also a two-time winner of Crystal Lake Publishing's monthly flash fiction contest. Currently, she is writing her first full length novel, half a dozen short stories, and a comic book series entitled *Siren's Song* that will be released later this year. Her newest tale, "Pretty on the Inside," is based on a true story. Visit her at dianaolney.com for updates on her latest nightmares.

Nathaniel Barrett is a rising High School Senior in the state of New Hampshire. His work has been recognized by the Scholastic Art & Writing Awards and will be published in the online magazine, *Bewildering Stories.* He writes primarily fiction, particularly in the genres of Science Fiction, Magical Realism, and just plain Realism. Whenever he is not writing, you will find him either reading, running, or spending time with his friends and family.

D.G. Ironside is an emerging Canadian author, content creator and persistent Improviser.

Printed in Great Britain
by Amazon